American POW Memoirs
from the Revolutionary War
through the Vietnam War

American POW Memoirs
from the Revolutionary War
through the Vietnam War

The Autobiography Seminar
Providence College
Spring Semester 2006

EDITED BY
JON ALEXANDER, O.P.

Eugene, Oregon

AMERICAN POW MEMOIRS FROM THE
REVOLUTIONARY WAR THROUGH THE VIETNAM WAR

Copyright © 2007 Jon Alexander, O.P. All rights reserved. Except for brief quotations in critical publications or reviews, no part of this book may be reproduced in any manner without prior written permission from the publisher. Write: Permissions, Wipf & Stock, 199 W. 8th Ave., Eugene, OR 97401.

ISBN 10: 1-59752-841-2
ISBN 13: 978-1-59752-841-2

Manufactured in the U.S.A.

Dedicated to
All the Prisoners of War

Contents

Acknowledgements / xi
Introduction by Jon Alexander, O.P. / 1

Revolution

Ethan Allen (1738–1789)
Narrative of Colonel Ethan Allen's Captivity (1779) / 15
—Stephen Vittorioso

Mexican-American War

John A. Scott (1824–1903)
Encarnacion Prisoners (1848) / 25
—Logan J. Reed

Civil War

Belle Boyd (1843–1900, Confederate)
Belle Boyd in Camp and Prison (1865) / 35
—Thomas Kettmer

Solon Hyde (1838–1920, Union)
A Captive of War (1900) / 43
—Emily Roach

John H. King (1843–19—, Confederate)
Three Hundred Days in a Yankee Prison (1904) / 51
—Christopher Emmens

Amos Stearns (1833–1912, Union)
Narrative of Amos E. Stearns (1887) / 57
—Jessica Pilkington

Spanish-American War

Richmond P. Hobson (1870–1937)
The Sinking of the Merrimac (1899) / 63
—Jason Coulombe

World War I

James N. Hall (1887–1951)
Flying with Chaucer (1930) / 71
—Lindsay Weber

World War II

William A. Berry (1915–2004), with James E. Alexander,
Prisoner of the Rising Sun (1993) / 79
—Michael Eng

Albert P. Clark (1913–)
*33 Months as a POW in Stalag Luft III:
A World War II Airman Tells His Story* (2004) / 85
—Kyle Casey

Dorothy S. Danner (1914–2001)
*What A Way to Spend a War: Navy Nurse POWs
in the Philippines* (1995) / 95
—Brigid McDonough

Korean War

William F. Dean (1914–1981)
*General Dean's Story as told to William L. Worden
by Major General William F. Dean* (1954) / 105
—Sarah Burke

Vietnam War

Jeremiah A. Denton, Jr. (1924–), with Ed Brandt
When Hell Was in Session (1976) / 111
—Sean Whalen

Contents

John McCain (1936–) with Mark Salter
Faith of My Fathers (1999) / 117
—Peter Farese

Books Cited / 125
Selected Sources Cited / 127

Acknowledgements

WE WISH to thank Sidone Smith, Julia Watson, and Dr. Dennis McCarthy, MD, for their advice in preparing this project; Matthew Dowling, History Department Chair, Providence College for allowing a seminar on American Veterans' memoirs to be offered; Owen D. Kubik, Kubik Fine Books Ltd., and Ron Randall, Randall House, for information on dust jackets; John Lawless, Nicholas Ingham, O.P. and Paul Seaver, O.P. for help with Latin quotations; Thomas McCreesh, O.P. for help with Greek quotations; Robert V. Aquilina, Judith Bellafaire, and Paul St Laurent for assistance with military questions, Dr. Yosef Ali, MD, for explaining injuries described in the memoirs, Francine Mancini and Janice Schuster for help in locating books and web sites.

Thanks are due the following copyright owners who were kind enough to grant permission to quote material in this volume.

From Ethan Allen, *Narrative of Colonel Ethan Allen's Captivity...*, by Ethan Allen (Philadelphia: Robert Bell, 1779), Early American Imprints Series I, #16182, used with the permission of News Bank/ Readex Inc. and the American Antiquarian Society.

From John H Scott, *Encarnacion Prisoners...*, by John H. Scott (Louisville: Prentice and Weissinger, 1848) courtesy of the Bancroft Library, Berkeley, California.

From Belle Boyd, *Belle Boyd in Camp and Prison...*, by Belle Boyd (New York: Blelock & Company, 1865) reprinted with a New Forward by Drew Gilpin Faust and a New Introduction by Sharon Kennedy-Nolle (Baton Rouge: Louisiana State University Press, 1998) courtesy of the Louisiana State University Press.

Acknowledgements

From Solon Hyde, *A Captive of War* by Solon Hyde (New York: McClure, Phillips & Co., 1900) is in the public domain. The instructor's copy of the original imprint was used.

From John H. King, *Three Hundred Days in a Yankee Prison...*, by John H. King (Atlanta: Jas P. Davis, 1904) is in the public domain. The electronic copy at the Library of Congress web site was used.

From Amos E. Stearns, *Narrative of Amos E. Stearns...*, by Amos E. Stearns (Worcester: Franklin P. Rice, Publisher, 1887) courtesy of LexusNexus Academic and Library Solutions, a division of Reed Elsevier Inc. (successor-in-interest to University Publications of America).

From Amos E. Stearns, *The Civil War Diary of Amos E. Stearns, a Prisoner at Andersonville*, edited by Leon Basile (East Brunswick, NJ: Associated University Presses, 1981). Copyright © 1981 by Associated University Presses, Inc. Quoted by permission of the Publisher.

From Richmond P. Hobson, "The Sinking of the 'Merrimac,'" by Richmond P. Hobson, *The Century Magazine* (December 1891-March 1899) courtesy of the Cornell University Library, Making of America Digital Collection.

From James Norman Hall, *Flying With Chaucer*, by James Norman Hall (Boston: Houghton Mifflin Company, 1930). Copyright © 1930 by James Norman Hall. Quoted by permission of Nancy Hall Rutgers.

From William A. Berry with James Edwin Alexander, *Prisoner of the Rising Sun*, by William A. Berry and James Edwin Alexander (Norman: University of Oklahoma Press, 1993). Copyright © 1993 by the University of Oklahoma Press, Norman, Publishing Division of the University. Quoted by permission of James Edwin Alexander.

From Albert P. Clark, *33 Months as a POW in Stalag Luft III: A World War II Airman Tells His Story*, by Albert P. Clark (Golden, CO: Fulcrum Publishing, 2004). Copyright © 2004 by Albert P. Clark. Quoted by permission of Fulcrum Publishing.

Acknowledgements

From Dorothy Still Danner, *What a Way to Spend a War*, by Dorothy Still Danner (Annapolis: Naval Institute Press, 1995). Copyright © 1995 by Dorothy Still Danner. Quoted by permission of Naval Institute Press.

From William F. Dean, *General Dean's Story as told to William L. Worden by Major General William F. Dean* (New York: The Viking Press, 1954). Copyright © by William F. Dean, renewed © 1982 by Mildred D. Dean. Used by permission of Viking Penguin, a division of Penguin Group (USA) Inc.

From Jeremiah A. Denton, Jr., with Ed Brandt, *When Hell Was in Session: A Personal Story of Survival as a POW in North Vietnam* (New York: Reader's Digest Press, 1976). Copyright © 1976 by Jeremiah A. Denton, Jr. and Edwin H. Brandt, Jr. Quoted by permission of Admiral Jeremiah A. Denton, Jr.

From John McCain with Mark Salter, *Faith of My Fathers* by John Mc Cain with Mark Salter (New York: Random House, Inc., 1999). Copyright © 1999 by John McCain and Mark Salter. Quoted by permission of Random House, Inc.

From Richard W. Turk, "Introduction," by Richard W. Turk to *The Sinking of the "Merrimac"* by Richmond P. Hobson (Annapolis: Naval Institute Press, 1987). Copyright © 1987 to the introduction and notes by the U. S. Naval Institute. Quoted by permission Naval Institute Press.

Introduction

Jon Alexander, O.P.

How These Fourteen Papers Came to Be Written

American POW Memoirs from the Revolutionary War through the Vietnam War is a collection of papers from an undergraduate seminar I offered during the spring semester 2006 at Providence College.[1] In the course of research during a sabbatical year (2004–2005) I noticed that there did not seem to be any collective examination of United States veterans' memoirs from more than one war, and I thought the topic of veterans' memoirs might make an interesting theme for a seminar.[2] In the course of planning the seminar, I decided it would provide more coherence for the students if they were required to write their papers on POW accounts.

The list of POW memoirs I compiled from which students selected memoirs for their papers was not a representative collection of United

---

[1] Providence College is a liberal arts college in Providence, Rhode Island founded by the Order of Preachers, a religious order in the Roman Catholic Church, of which I am a member. The paper on *The Sinking of the Merrimac* was written by a graduate student. With the exception of first year students, the seminar was open to any student. It was not an honors seminar. For the information of readers I should note than my military experience is limited to two years of Army ROTC.

[2] I think "memoir" is the best way to describe the fourteen texts considered here because, with the possible exception of John McCain's *Faith of My Fathers*, the texts describe an episode in their authors' lives. Philippe Lejeune, "The Autobiographical Pact," in *On Autobiography*, ed. Paul John Eakin, trans. Katherine Leary (Minneapolis: University of Minnesota Press, 1989), p. 4 defines autobiography as a "Retrospective prose narrative written by a real person concerning his own existence, where the focus is his own life, in particular the story of his personality." The texts considered here are retrospective prose narratives written by real persons (whose existence can be confirmed in newspapers and other sources) concerning something that happened *to* them, in particular their internment as POWs. These texts focus on an episode in their authors' lives, but only indirectly and partially on the stories of their personalities.

States POW narratives in any sense.³ Only memoirs from nine major wars, from the Revolutionary War through the Vietnam War, written by authors who had some identifiable military connection were considered. Only memoirs that were available to the students through the College Library, through purchase, or through a copy obtained from another library collection could be considered. A list of POW memoirs available for the nine major wars (Revolutionary War, War of 1812, Mexican-American War, Civil War, Spanish-American War, World War I, World War II, Korean War, and Vietnam War) was included in the seminar syllabus. In those cases where more than one text was available for a particular war the students could choose among the available texts for the seminar paper.⁴

I prepared a data inventory form for the students to use to collect information from the memoirs, and a basic outline for the first draft.⁵ In the course of writing the second and third drafts, the students and I decided to retain the basic outline as topical subheadings in the papers. Each of the following papers, therefore, contains seven topical sections: (1) the text, (2) the author, (3) framing the narrative, (4) structure of the narrative, (5) construction of the narrative, (6) contents of the narrative, and (7) conclusion. As these topical subheadings indicate, the focus of the seminar, and of the fourteen papers here, is on the memoirs as texts—not on exactly what happened.⁶ These papers offer some thoughts about how some fourteen American authors described the experience of being a POW and some tentative opinions about how American soldiers have constructed a POW memoir, but these papers do not offer any information about persons or internments that rise above the anecdotal or impressionistic level.

---

³ Alex Vernon's essay, "No Genre's Land: The Problem of Genre in War Memoirs and Military Autobiography," in *Arms and the Self: War, the Military, and Autobiographical Writing*, ed. Alex Vernon (Kent, OH: Kent State University Press, 2005) 1–34 indicates the wide range of military life writings including POW accounts that should be considered in developing a representative bibliography.

⁴ Excluded here, for example, are POW memoirs from Colonial wars, wars with Native American Tribes, the Tripolitan War, and memoirs by civilian POWs. The student who wrote a paper on the POW memoir from the War of 1812 chose not to revise the paper for publication and it is not included here.

⁵ The seminar syllabus is available at the History Department page at the Providence College web site under my name. In the course of searching for American POW memoirs, I noticed enough memoirs by POWs held by the United States to suspect that memoirs by POWs held by the United States could be a topic for a scholarly meeting. Of course, POWs in the Civil War were held in American (Confederate or Union) internment camps.

⁶ "Exactly what happened" is a paraphrase of Leopold von Ranke, "Preface:" *Histories of Latin and Germanic Peoples from 1494–1514*, trans. Fritz Stern, in *The Varieties of History from Voltaire to the Present*, ed. Fritz Stern (New York: Vintage Books, 1973) 59.

Introduction

Narrative Construction

The fourteen POW memoirs considered here basically correspond with Robert C. Doyle's description of the narrative contour of American POW narratives in *Voices from Captivity*. Doyle notes seven characteristic "event-scenarios" in American POW accounts: (1) pre-capture autobiography, (2) capture, (3) death march/remove, (4) prison landscape, (5) resistance: survival or assimilation, (6) release and repatriation, (7) lament.[7] The memoirs of Ethan Allen, James Norman Hall, Richmond Hobson, Solon Hyde, John A. Scott and Amos Stearns have no pre-capture autobiography. There are no descriptions of post repatriation experiences in the memoirs of Solon Hyde and John A. Scott, and the description of post-repatriation experiences is short in the accounts of Ethan Allen, William A. Berry, William F. Dean, James Norman Hall, Richmond Hobson, and Amos Stearns.[8] Albert P. Clark includes post repatriation information throughout his memoir. Belle Boyd, Dorothy Still Danner, Jeremiah A. Denton Jr., John H. King and John McCain describe their post repatriation experience, but only in King's memoir, and in the memoirs of Danner and Boyd to a much lesser extent, is a sense of loss and enduring trauma mentioned. McCain remarks: "In the years after I came home, I never suffered from flashbacks or post-traumatic stress syndrome, as it is clinically termed."[9] With the exceptions of Doyle's first event-scenario (pre-capture autobiography) and his last event-scenario (lament), the fourteen POW memoirs considered here contain the "event-scenarios" that Doyle describes.

Many memoirs have an element of collective authorship because many authors revise some of their recollections and polish their writing after sharing parts of their memoirs with family, friends, and editors before publication.[10] Four of the authors considered here acknowledge collaborators on the title page: Berry, Denton, and McCain describe their collaboration with the word "with," and Dean describes his collaboration with the

---

[7] Robert C. Doyle, *Voices from Captivity: Interpreting the American POW Narrative* (Lawrence: University of Kansas Press, 1994), chapter 4, 81–88.

[8] There is an epilogue in Berry's memoir with post repatriation information about the author and other POWs mentioned in the memoir. This is written mainly in the third person. Scott's memoir ends abruptly before he gets home.

[9] John McCain with Mark Salter, *Faith of My Fathers* (New York: Random House, 1999) 221, hereafter cited as McCain. I read Boyd's sense of loss to arise more from the death of her husband and to the defeat of the Confederacy than to her POW experiences.

[10] For an excellent analysis of how life writings come to be written see, Sidonie Smith and Julia Watson, *Reading Autobiography: A Guide for the Interpretation of Life Narratives* (Minneapolis: University of Minnesota Press, 2001), 49–81.

phrase, "as told to." Boyd's memoir contains a lengthy section attributed to her husband, Samuel Hardinge.[11] The other memoirs, with the exception of Scott's *Encarnacion*, where the author's name does not appear on the title page, are presented as the work of a single author.[12]

Only one of the memoirs considered here, James Norman Hall's *Flying with Chaucer*, was written by a professional writer who made a living by writing.[13] The fact that all but one of the authors considered here could be classified as amateurs is not to say that their memoirs lack sophistication or subtlety. Most of the authors exhibit facility in constructing recollected conversations, in selecting illustrative episodes, and in writing persuasive argumentation that makes a point. The quotations and allusions in the memoirs indicate that these authors were not unread, and it appears fairly likely that all of the authors were familiar with the *Bible*, a text which, among many other things, is a great compendium of several narrative styles and literary strategies.[14]

Most of the authors of memoirs considered here were officers at the time of their internment.[15] Belle Boyd, who was a spy, did not have an official rank or an official connection with the Confederate Army, but she claims to have received a ". . . commission as Captain and honorary Aide-de-camp to 'Stonewall' Jackson . . . ."[16] King, Scott, Stearns, and Hyde were privates.[17] Two of the officers were airmen, but because the Air Force as a separate branch was established after their time of service, they were officially in the Army. Five of the authors were in the Navy and eight were in the Army (King was in the Confederate Army). I regret that the circum-

---

[11] Hardinge's part is not acknowledged on the title page, Belle Boyd, *Belle Boyd in Camp and Prison* (Baton Rouge: Louisiana State University Press, 1998) 54, hereafter cited as Boyd.

[12] Because a good editor or collaborator can help authors who are unaccustomed to writing to express what they wish to communicate more coherently, it should not be presumed that memoirs that mention an editor or a collaborator are necessarily less authentic than memoirs self-published by the author.

[13] James Norman Hall, *Flying with Chaucer* (Boston: Houghton Mifflin, 1930), hereafter cited as Hall.

[14] Robert Alter, *The Art of Biblical Narrative* (New York: Basic Books, 1981) provides an excellent consideration of the complexities of biblical writing.

[15] A chart at the end of this introduction lists the rank of all the authors at the time of their internments.

[16] Boyd, 146.

[17] Hyde's rank is not mentioned in his memoir, but an Ohio Genealogical Site indicates that his beginning rank was private and his ending rank was corporal (a non-commissioned officer below the rank of sergeant). I am assuming Hyde was promoted after his release from Andersonville.

stances of collecting and selecting memoirs resulted in the omission of a POW account by a Marine.[18]

The Description of Internment

Any sort of coerced confinement is inherently unpleasant, but even a benevolent internment is hard time for most fighting men and women who would prefer to stay in the fight. There are two factors, mentioned in the fourteen memoirs considered here, that appear to correlate with how tolerable or how intolerable a POW internment experience is described. These two factors are rank and the perceived distance between POW's and their captors.[19]

The memories of privates Hyde, King, Scott, and Stearns mention no special treatment. Stearns and Hyde explain that they survived Andersonville because of help from friends who were POWs and some lucky breaks.[20] King reports that he was saved from going to the dreaded internment hospital because another POW, who King had previously nursed, nursed King when he got sick.[21] Scott recalls that his Mexican captors gave the POW officers a higher allowance for food and necessities than they gave the enlisted men.[22] Dean reports that he got special treatment because he was a general.[23] Ethan Allen complains, as if he were describing an atrocious offense, that all the POWs ". . . were locked up in one common large

---

[18] The omission of a Marine POW memoir is my fault, and it results from my scramble to find POW memoirs from all the major wars. It was only when I typed the syllabus that I noticed that there was only one account by a Marine POW, James P. S. Devereux's *Wake Island*, but this memoir is mainly about the defense of Wake Island and Devereux's description of his POW experience constitutes only about six percent of the text.

[19] The importance of rank was first called to my attention by Samuel Hynes, *The Soldiers' Tale: Bearing Witness to Modern War* (New York: Penguin Books, 1998) 254. Hynes chapter six, "Agents and Suffers is an outstanding discussion of POW narratives.

[20] Amos E. Stearns, *Narrative of Amos E. Stearns . . .* (Worcester: Franklin P. Rice, Publisher, 1887), 26 (on page 26 Stearns describes his capture as a "misfortune"), hereafter cited as Stearns. Solon Hyde, *A Captive of War . . .* (New York: McClure, Phillips & Co., 1900) 242–244, hereafter cited as Hyde.

[21] John H. King, *Three Hundred Days in a Yankee Prison . . .* (Atlanta: Jas P. Davis, 1904) 84–79, hereafter cited as King. The Library of Congress copy scanned to their web site was used.

[22] [John H. Scott], *Encarnacion Prisoners . . .* (Louisville: Prentice and Weissinger, 1848) 49–50, hereafter cited as Scott.

[23] William F. Dean, *General Dean's Story as told to William L. Worden . . .* (New York: The Viking Press, 1954) 91, 115.

room, without regard to rank, education or any other accomplishment."²⁴ Hobson recalled his concern for his men because as an officer he was given different quarters and didn't know what was happening to them.²⁵ Because ten of the fourteen POW memoirs considered here were written by officers, it is possible that the composite picture of internment derived from these texts is more favorable than would have been the case had a majority of the memoirs been written by privates. The memoirs of Dean, Denton and McCain, however, describe the difficult internment that POW officers may experience when their captors seek to force propaganda statements from higher ranking captives.²⁶

The greater the perceived distance between POWs and their captors the more likely that internment will be described as brutish. The distance resulting from differences of language and culture are described as producing miscommunication, discomfort and hardship. Language differences are not described as significant because of the presence of translators, restrictions on communication between POWs and captors in many situations, and the facility of many of the authors considered here in nonverbal communication. Denton mentions a brief exchange in French, but on another occasion he is able to communicate with some Vietnamese construction workers with a glance.²⁷ Berry describes a remarkable instance of muddling through cultural and linguistic barriers. He recalls that the Japanese interrogating him about his escape unexpectedly became sympathetic when he took a photograph of his mother from his pocket and blurted out to them, "I wanted to go home to my mother."²⁸ Dean complains about Korean kimchee, Clark grumbles about German kohlrabi, and several authors describe their annoyance with unfamiliar etiquette.²⁹ In many cases the de-

---

²⁴ Ethan Allen, *Narrative of Colonel Allen's Captivity* . . . (Philadelphia: Robert Bell, 1779) 24, hereafter cited as Allen.

²⁵ Richmond P. Hobson, "The Sinking of the 'Merrimac,'" *The Century Magazine*, 57 (February, 1899): 584, 590 (*The Century Magazine* is on line at the Making of America site).

²⁶ Dean, 132–135; Jeremiah A. Denton, Jr. with Ed Brandt, *When Hell Was in Session* (New York: Reader's Digest Press, 1976), 28–33, hereafter cited as Denton; McCain, 192, 199–200, 282. Samuel Hardinge claims that the other POWs dropped their plan to toss him in a blanket when they learned that he was Belle Boyd's husband, Boyd, 240.

²⁷ Denton, 17, 189, 91–92.

²⁸ William A. Berry with James Edwin Alexander, *Prisoner of the Rising Sun* (Norman: University of Oklahoma Press, 1993), 70, 142, hereafter cited as Berry.

²⁹ Dean, 243 (he grows to like kimchee); Albert P. Clark, *33 Months as a POW in Stalag Luft III: A World War II Airman Tells His Story* (Golden, CO: Fulcrum Publishing, 2004) 49, hereafter cited as Clark; Berry, 146; Dorothy Still Danner, *What a Way to Spend a War*

scription of internment hardships that arise from linguistic and cultural distance between POWs and captors is constructed more like the awkward moments in travel accounts than like the description of atrocities in survivors' accounts.

Rebellion, however, is described as producing a distance between captors and POWs that trumps even similarities of culture and language. Boyd frequently complains of rude and relentless Yankee jailers who are kept in check only by her steel magnolia assertive gentility. Allen describes the hostile behavior of several British captors and he relishes the occasions when he is able to "come Yankee" over them. Hyde, Stearns and King describe atrocities and inhuman treatment from guards who had recently been fellow citizens. Rebellion can lead loyalists to view rebels as criminals and rebels to view loyalists as tyrants. Enemies who are perceived as criminals or tyrants may not deserve good treatment when interned or when described in a memoir.[30]

Ideological differences, like rebellion, can distance captors and POWs. Clark mentions the effects of Fascism, but he does not describe it as having a significant effect on his internment. Denton and McCain recall unpleasant incidents that result from being captives of Communists. Although Dean comes to admire some of the human qualities of his captors, he describes several occasions when ideological differences lead to unpleasant situations. Denton's description of ideological differences is intense. He recalls, "Also becoming clear to me was the infinite difference between the heartless, mindless, and Godless nature of the Democratic Republic of Vietnam and the United States of America." For McCain internment is described more like a contest of will than a contest of ideology.[31]

Military professionalism (chivalry, gallantry, or old regime etiquette) and an attitude of soldierly fatalism about the fortunes of war (today's captor could be tomorrow's POW) are described as factors that mitigate the distance between captor and POW. Allen recalls the remark of a captor who treated Allen with particular kindness that "this is a mutable world, and one gentleman never knows but it may be in his power to help another."[32] Danner remembers that another POW, Mitch, remarked about

---

... (Thorndike, ME: G. K. Hall & Co., 1997), 110–111, 118, hereafter cited as Danner; Denton, 36; McCain, 227; Denton notes that the first leg irons in which he was placed " . . . were leftovers from the French, and much heavier than the ones the North Vietnamese later used, Denton, 63. Denton had previously mentioned that his ancestry was French (11).

[30] Boyd, 94–95, 127, 133, 141, 161; Allen, 12, 15, 17–18; Hyde, 71, 59, 67, 121, 188; Stearns, 14, 45; King, 76, 80–82.

[31] Clark, 48–49, 53, 55; Dean, 291–292; Denton, 69; McCain, 207.

[32] Allen, 26.

one internment camp commander, Lt. Col. Kimura, "Jap or not, there goes the gentleman."³³ Clark recalls that the internment camp commandant, Colonel Friedrich Wilhelm Lindeiner-Wildau, ". . . was an impressive old gentleman . . . and an officer of the old school." Clark adds almost regretfully, "Few of us knew about or appreciated his efforts to keep the camp from being taken over and managed by Heinrich Himmler and his wretched Gestapo."³⁴ Hyde mentions the medical professionalism of several Confederate army surgeons.³⁵ Hobson, describing the courteous behavior of his captors, recalls that "Captain Acosta gallantly opened the conversation by saying that there was no reason why officers engaged in honorable warfare, though opposing to their utmost in battle, might not be the best of friends."³⁶

There are five factors that seem not to correlate with how internment is described in the fourteen accounts considered here.³⁷ The age of the author at the time of internment is not decisive because Allen and Denton, both about 41, describe harsh internment, but King who was 21 offers a similar description. Relatively pleasant internment is described by Scott (22), Boyd (20), Hobson (28), Clark (29) and Hall (30). Stearns' memoir suggests that POWs who had hard lives before internment might tend to describe internment more favorably than those who were accustomed to a higher standard of living, but Hyde, a physician's son, describes Andersonville with less venom than King, a small plantation owner's son, employs to castigate Camp Chase. Clark, Hall, and Hobson, all educated middle-class men, describe mild internment. Victories by a POW's side in war do not correlate with better internment treatment. Allen and Denton note that internment conditions improved with the success of American arms, but Clark and Berry note the opposite. The length of time from repatriation to publication does not correlate with how internment is described. King, who published 48 years after repatriation, and Allen, who published one

---

³³ Danner, 217.

³⁴ Clark, 54–55.

³⁵ Hyde, 118, 104.

³⁶ Richmond P. Hobson, "The Sinking of the 'Merrimac,'" *The Century Magazine* 57 (February, 1899): 580. One factor that may correlate with poor internment treatment is the poverty of the captors. Dean, for example, notes poor food, but also that he was fed better than North Korean troops, but poverty of the captors does not explain the starving times Allen described. Of course, to consider this correlation it would be necessary to have information about the specific economic conditions at the time and the place of each internment.

³⁷ Information considered in this paragraph is summarized in a chart at the end of the introduction.

year after repatriation, both bitterly castigate their captors, but Scott, who published a year after repatriation, and Clark, who published 59 years after repatriation, describe their captors as basically decent. It would seem that the way internment is described is in part related to the putatively empirical factors about the character of the internment and the author who was experiencing it, but other factors such as an author's perspective at the time a POW memoir is written and the type of memoir (or basic memoir plot) an author seeks to write are also significant.

Some Narrative Features

There are four basic narrative plots with some elements of hybridity that are characteristic of the fourteen memoirs considered here: (1) a narrative that demonizes the enemy, (2) an account of learning and growth through adversity which is similar to a coming of age narrative, (3) a survivor's account, and (4) an ironic account.[38] Demonizing the enemy is the basic plot of the memoirs of Allen, Boyd, Denton, Hyde, and King. Denton and Hyde, and to a lesser extent King, describe individual acts of kindness, sometimes even from internment guards, but to my reading these exceptional instances of decency primarily serve to make the indictment of the enemy more credible. Boyd's memoir demonizes the Yankees, but her indictment is muted by two countervailing narrative themes: her effort to write a book that will sell in the North, and her desire to illustrate how her southern gentility trumped Yankee meanness. Allen's memoir demonizes the British, especially British loyalists, but, like Boyd's memoir, Allen's contains a countervailing theme: the illustration of how a Yankee gentleman can trump British tyrants. Hall's memoir has a basically ironic plot, and Clark's memoir describes an experience of growth through adversity with humor and irony. The basic theme of McCain's memoir is personal growth through adversity. The memoirs of Hobson and Scott are also basically descriptions of learning experiences but these authors relate their experiences more like an adventure story in which authors learn by visiting strange places that they sometimes describe like a travelogue. Danner's memoir is a survivor's account of enduring punishing experiences. The theme of survival is also prominent in the memoirs of Berry and Dean, but in Berry's memoir the struggle to survive is told with a degree of humor that gives an

---

[38] I tell my students that a plot in life writing resembles a plan for writing a resume. A resume plan guides us in selecting what to leave out, what to put in, and what to explain, but applications for different jobs may require different resumes with different resume plans. Memoirs are not transparent windows on an author's life. Most of the time, memoirs, like resumes, are performative constructions.

ironic tone to his description of his POW experience, whereas in Dean's memoir his apologetic agenda of explaining how a general was captured because he became separated from his army holds an equal prominence with the story of his survival.

Self-presentations

An author's self-presentation in a memoir is rarely completely consistent, and the fourteen POW authors considered here present themselves in different ways at different points in their memoirs. For example, selves presented as very soldierly and fiercely resistant to their captors may be presented, on occasion, as beleaguered or as the recipients of gratuitous lucky breaks that are unconnected with their frequently described soldierly efforts. In the main, however, the authors present themselves consistently enough that the fourteen self-presentations considered here may be classified into one of four styles: (1) a beleaguered self, (2) a distanced self, (3) a fortunate self, (4) a soldierly self.[39]

Danner presents herself as a beleaguered POW nurse: malnourished, overwhelmed, caught in a tangle of unanticipated and complex relationships, and yet still struggling to care for the sick and injured. Danner's self-construction occasionally laughs at her situation, but Danner does not employ humor to distance her narrative persona from the adversity that beleaguers her. King's self-construction is similar to Danner's, but King's narrative persona carries polemical freight that is absent in Danner's memoir. Danner's memoir seems intended to memorialize the heroism of the Navy nurses and other American military personnel held in the Philippines, but King's memoir is intended to reveal the hypocrisy of Yankee criticism of Confederate internment camps by illustrating the horrors of a Union POW camp. King's POW persona is beleaguered by relentless Yankee vindictiveness: too terrorized to attempt escape, too weakened by malnutrition to resist, and too wracked by illness to fight.[40]

---

[39] The classification, "beleaguered self" is borrowed from Diane Bjorklund, *Interpreting the Self: Two Hundred Years of American Autobiography* (Chicago: University of Chicago Press, 1998), 124–57.

[40] Perhaps Danner and King are the only memoirs considered here that devote more than a few sentences to describing their lives after repatriation because the trauma lasts for a beleaguered self (both the self constructed in a memoir and the "actual" self constructed in part from memory). Perhaps keeping up the fight helps fighting men and women cope with the horrors of internment by enabling them to sustain their identities and avoid a wrenching reconceptionalizing of themselves as victims. Denton and McCain, who present soldierly selves in their memoirs, praise the Military Code of Conduct that requires POWs to resist, while Berry, who does not present a soldierly self, questions the wisdom of the

Introduction

Scott, Stearns, and Hall present a self that is distanced from the experience of internment, but the distancing of the self is achieved in different ways. Stearns' self-presentation is so consistently descriptive and reserved that Stearns seems like an anthropologist observing himself from a distance. Scott's memoir, which never uses the first person singular and includes his name only at the end in a list of American prisoners, presents no distinguishable self at all. Scott writes as an almost invisible witness for the group of POWs captured at Encarnacion, Mexico. Hall's almost picaresque construction of his POW experience as a sort of read through Chaucer's *Canterbury Tales* distances his narrative persona from internment by presenting himself as if he just happened to be at a strange location reading his Chaucer.

Three authors construct a persona that is occasionally beleaguered and soldierly but more frequently survives through lucky breaks. Hobson, who describes his internment as relatively pleasant and his captors as gallant, constructs himself as the beneficiary of many gratuitous kindnesses. Hyde survives Andersonville because a friend arranges for his transfer to the pharmacy.[41] Berry notes that his military training was so inadequate that he didn't know how to load a cartridge clip, but luckily his legal training as a civilian and a picture of his mother unexpectedly save him from death.[42]

The most common self-construction presented in the fourteen memoirs is a soldierly self. This persona is found in the memoirs of Allen, Boyd, Clark, Dean, Denton, and McCain. The soldierly persona resists captors, plans escapes, may be crushed temporarily by brutal punishments and torture but bounces back to resist again.[43] Even though internment conditions were tolerable and he was unaware of any Army directive that POWs should attempt escape, Clark describes spending much of his time as a POW planning escape tunnels, gathering intelligence, supervising the making of false papers, maps, compasses and other prohibited activities.[44] Boyd recalls hanging a half-length portrait of Jefferson Davis in her Union internment cell with the inscription, "Three cheers for Jeff. Davis and the Southern

---

Code's directions. Ben Shephard's chapter "The Culture of Trauma," in his book *A War of Nerves: Soldiers and Psychiatrists in the Twentieth Century* (Cambridge: Harvard University Press, 2001), 385–99, examines this issue.

[41] Hyde, 243–44. I wonder if Hyde's self-construction as buffeted by chance may not serve to intensify his characterization of the antagonist of his memoir, the Confederacy, as an intentional and diabolical conspiracy.

[42] Berry, 15, 162–72, 100, 142.

[43] I am borrowing the term, "bounce back," from Denton, 105.

[44] Clark, x, 59.

Confederacy!"⁴⁵ Allen recalls that ". . . a lieutenant among the Tories, insulted me . . . and spit in my face; upon which, (tho' I was hand-cuffed), I sprang at him with both hands, and knocked him partly down . . . ."⁴⁶ When a North Korean colonel threatened Dean with torture using pressurized water, Dean replied, "That sounds good to me. The shape I'm in you won't have to use much pressure. I think that'll kill me quickly. That sounds all right."⁴⁷ McCain recalls, "Whenever I emerged from the interrogation room after a few hours or a few days of punishment, I tried to make a show of my indifference to my circumstances. Whether I walked on my own accord or was dragged back to my cell, I always shouted greetings to the prisoners whose cells I passed, smiled, and flashed a thumbs-up."⁴⁸ Denton recalls that when an interrogator gave him a night to consider changing his mind about writing a statement confessing war crimes, Denton ". . . concluded that he was trying to provide me with a face-saving way to give in early during the torture the next day, by consoling myself that I had done enough to withstand the starvation treatment. He succeeded only in increasing my resolve."⁴⁹

Concluding Comments

All the POW memoirs considered here describe food and housing, captors, health, depression, homesickness, and the struggle to survive, but I think it would be unwise to make generalizations about American POW narratives on the basis of fourteen memoirs from eight different wars.⁵⁰ Every POW

---

⁴⁵ Boyd, 139.
⁴⁶ Allen, 13.
⁴⁷ Dean, 155.
⁴⁸ McCain, 246.

⁴⁹ Denton, 87. The construction of the soldierly self in the memoirs of Allen, Boyd, Clark, Dean, Denton, and McCain is rather consistent. For example, similar incidents are described and similar dialogues with captors and other POWs are constructed in ways that are often nearly alike. Perhaps there is something like a literary model for a POW soldierly self derived from patriotic legends (e.g., Nathan Hale), martyrologies (e.g., "Foxe's Book of Martyrs") and scripture (e.g., Sampson, Daniel, Shadrach, Meshach, Abednego, the mother and her seven sons [2 Maccabees, 8], and Paul) that provides a basic characterization for this self-construction.

⁵⁰ My reading of these fourteen POW memoirs suggests that an examination of the nicknames the POWs give to captors and internment locations, and the intertextual references (allusions, quotations, and modeling) in the memoirs would make a more interesting study than the description of food and housing. Are nicknames more likely to be mentioned in twentieth-century memoirs where authors describe themselves as soldierly, as is the case with the fourteen memoirs considered here?

memoir describes an experience of adversity, but how each narrative of adversity is told is different in its own way.[51] The fourteen papers presented here provide information about fourteen POW memoirs and some hints about how those narratives are constructed, but no attempt has been made to go beyond the narratives to consider the events, the issues, or the people the narratives describe.

American POW Memoirs from the Revolutionary War through the Vietnam War was made possible through the dedicated perseverance of fourteen students. Their achievement is all the more impressive in light of the many conflicting demands on their time. Every effort has been made to verify the citations, to check the quotations, and to eliminate errors from this text.[52] The thanks of all the participants in this project go to the many friends, family, and colleagues who read over the manuscript for mistakes. We apologize for any errors that have slipped through. If it were very easy for us humans to see our errors and to correct them readily, there might not be many wars or many POWs or many POW memoirs to study. It was the unanimous agreement of all the contributors to this book that in the unlikely event that a book comprised of undergraduate papers earned any royalties they would be donated to the International Red Cross (ICRC), an organization with a mission to assist all POWs.

---

[51] I am paraphrasing the beginning of Tolstoy's *Anna Karenina* with the intention of implying that POW internments are not the only experiences of confinement about which memoirs are written.

[52] In the process of commenting on and editing the students' papers I tried to respect the students' style of writing and to limit myself to raising questions about their interpretations of the memoirs. The papers, therefore, are not uniform and in some cases contain missteps and lapses. I thought it would spoil the fun of learning if I became an editorial martinet. Besides, now that my students know about POW memoirs I can't be too demanding or they might write a memoir that described my seminar as a sort of internment!

Table of Information about the Authors

Name	Rank when interned	Approximate age when interned	Approximate duration of internment	Approximate time between repatriation and publication
Allen	Colonel, Army	41	32 months	1 year
Berry	Ensign, Navy	27	34 months	48 years
Boyd	Spy	20	4 months	1 year
Clark	Lt. Colonel, Army	29	33 months	59 years
Danner	Ensign, Navy	28	34 months	50 years
Dean	General, Army	46	39 months	1 year
Denton	Captain, Navy	41	92 months	3 years
Hall	Captain, Army	30	15 months	12 years
Hobson	Lieutenant, Navy	28	1 month	5 months
Hyde	Private, Army	25	17 months	35 years
King	Private, Army	21	10 months	48 years
McCain	Lt. Commander, Navy	31	68 months	26 years
Scott	Private, Army	22	10 months	1 year
Stearns	Private, Army	31	11 months	22 years

Ethan Allen:
Colonel Ethan Allen's Captivity

A Revolutionary War Memoir

STEPHEN VITTORIOSO

The Text

ETHAN ALLEN'S *The Narrative of Colonel Ethan Allen*[1] is an autobiography that depicts the hardships and adventures of Ethan Allen's captivity by British troops. Allen's narrative appeared in a six-part serialization in the 1779 November edition of *The Pennsylvania Packet*, where the narrative became an immediate bestseller.[2] The first edition came in Philadelphia 1779 by Robert Bell, printed in double columns. There are no major discrepancies between the 1779 Bell edition and the 1779 *The Pennsylvania Packet* serialization. There are, however, a few minor differences in punctu-

---

[1] The full title of Allen's narrative is *A Narrative of Colonel Ethan Allen's Captivity, From the Time of his being taken by the British, near Montreal, on the 25th Day of September, in the Year 1775; to the Time of his exchange, on the 6th day of May, 1778: Containing His Voyages and Travels.*

[2] Allen's narratives appeared in The Pennsylvania Packet on November 9, 11, 13, 16, 20, and 25. There are a number of secondary sources that list The Pennsylvania Packet's serialization of Allen's narrative in March 1779. This is, however, incorrect. *The National Index of American Imprints Through 1800*, compiled by Clifford K. Shipton and James E. Mooney, 2 vols. (Worcester, MA: The American Antiquarian Society and Barre Publishers, 1969), cites four additional publications of Allen's Narrative before 1801. A search using The Early American Newspaper: Series One search engine did not return any reviews of Allen's Narrative. A search in America: History and Life and The MLA Index (April 16, 2006) indicates that three articles on Allen's Narrative were published between 1970 and 2006. There is also a dissertation by Robert Doddridge Sturr, "Soldiers Stories of the American Revolution: Autobiographies, Politics, and the Patriotic Ideal," Ph.D. Dissertation, University of Southern California, 1998, and a chapter in a book by Stephen Carl Arch. *After Franklin: The Emergence of Autobiography in Post-Revolutionary America 1780–1830* (Hanover and London: University Press of New England, 2001).

ation in *The Pennsylvania Packet*, and the *Packet* series does not include the narrative's ending.[3] The autobiography's intended audience is the American people and the text seems intended to foster American patriotism.

The Author

Ethan Allen (1738–1789),[4] frontier revolutionary leader and author of the first deistic work by an American, was born in Litchfield, Connecticut, and was the eldest child of Joseph and Mary Baker Allen. Allen's brother, Ira, is famous in the early history of Vermont. In 1775, Allen's father died, so Allen took care of his mother and siblings. As a young man, Allen always displayed interest in the military, and he became briefly involved in the Colonial Militia of the French and Indian War. Allen's aggressive persona lead to his departure from both Sudbury, Massachusetts (1765) and Northampton, Massachusetts (1767). In 1770, Allen moved to the disputed Green Mountains in New York, and founded the Green Mountain Boys in 1771. Allen also published many newspaper articles about land ownership. Allen married Mary Brownson and had five children. Alongside Benedict Arnold in 1775, Allen's men ransacked and captured Fort Ticonderoga, but Allen claims credit for this attack. After this accomplishment, Allen commanded a small group of men to seize and capture Montreal, Quebec, but miscommunication caused Allen's capture by the British forces. The British then brought him to England before paroling him in New York. After his captivity, Allen moved back to Vermont, where he became heavily active in Vermont politics, attempting to convince Congress to allow Vermont statehood, and he operated as commander in chief of Vermont's military forces.

After Allen's military and political careers, Allen identified himself as a philosophical man by writing a book, *Reason the Only Oracle of Man* in 1785. In this publication, Allen wrote "to show the logical fallacies of Christianity" and "to put forth a deistic religion of nature."[5] The outcome of this book was not in Allen's favor, as Americans repelled such religious thoughts and explanations. In 1783, Allen's wife died, but he later remarried in the same year. At the age of 51, in the year 1783, Allen died of a stroke.

---

[3] *The Narrative of Colonel Ethan Allen* saw publication in 1779 by William Mentz of Philadelphia. There are no contemporary reviews in the journals.

[4] Biographical information about Allen is from Michael Bellesiles "Ethan Allen," *American National Biography*. Eds. John A. Garraty and Mark C. Carnes, 24 vols. (New York: Oxford University Press, 1999), 1:309–10.

[5] Bellesiles, *American National Biography*, 310.

Ethan Allen: Colonel Ethan Allen's Captivity

Framing of the Narrative

On the cover of *The Narrative of Colonel Ethan Allen* is the narrative's full title, and a disclaimer that reads "Interspersed with some Political Observations," which seem directed against the Tories. The title page also includes the reason for the narrative's publication: "For the Curious in all Nations" for "Ten Paper Dollars," and the publisher's name, Robert Bell of Third Street in Philadelphia.[6] On the title page, Allen includes an excerpt from the poem, *American Independence* by Freneau:

> When God From Chaos gave this World to be,
> Man then He form'd, and from'd him to be free.

This poem indicates God's notion that Man is free, and never captured. Allen includes this poem to show the American public that they are free, especially at a time during the Revolutionary War era. The last page of the Narrative is filled with an advertisement for a Spelling book published by Bell.

Structure of the Narrative

The trajectory of Allen's narrative is chronological. Following a sentence and a half portraying his patriotic feelings, Allen begins his account with his surprise May 10, 1775 capture on Fort Ticonderoga. After this capture, the narrative turns into an adventure because the British troops take him to numerous countries across the Atlantic Ocean. Allen's captivity takes him from Montreal to England via a ship to his imprisonment at Pendennis Castle. From his imprisonment, he sets sail on a ship to Ireland before sailing to Cape Fear and New York in America. His captivity continues to Halifax, and then returns to Long Island for his parole. *The Narrative of Colonel Ethan Allen* ends on a very positive note with Allen's parole in New York, his visit to General Washington at Valley Forge, and his return to Vermont as a hero. The description of Allen's visit to Washington and his reception in Vermont serve to confirm his repatriated status, and his incorporation into the ranks of American patriots. This supports his claim

---

[6] Because of the difficulty in reading the Bell edition, I used the 1961 Corinth Edition of Allen's Narrative as both a supplement and a trot. This edition has an Introduction by Brooke Hindle, associate professor of History at New York University. In this introduction, Hindle provides an overview of the narrative, and identifies many significant omissions from Allen's autobiography. An example of a significant omission is that Allen does not detail his imprisonment on Long Island. After Hindle's three paged Introduction, there is a two page Preface to the Walpole Edition, 1807.

that he is the same man he was before his 975 days of captivity.[7] Allen's narrative contains one flashback, and the narrative does not have a defined turning point.[8]

Construction of the Narrative

Allen constructs his narrative in a plain and simple writing style with little use of quotations. Most of his sentences are long with distinct, crisp detail because Allen tries to make his captivity conditions sound worse than what he experienced. Allen does not include any positive descriptions of the Tories; instead, Allen constructs the Tories to represent Hell on earth created by men corrupted by false political faith.[9] Allen particularly mentions the meanness of one Tory named Brook Watson on *The Adamant*. Allen emphasizes that Watson was "a man of malicious and cruel disposition with that spirit of bitterness, which is the peculiar characteristic of Tories, when they have the friends of American in their power, measuring their loyalty to the English king, by the barbarity, fraud, and deceit which they exercise towards the Whigs."[10] Through out his captivity, Allen kept a very positive attitude, especially because of fine food and drink and friendship. Allen also includes a document called Burgoyne's Proclamation,[11] to show the hypocrisy of England, and the Proclamation initiates a three-page catharsis where Allen writes his "true feelings" towards England. One of the major themes in Allen's narrative is the theme of mutability of the world.[12] Allen does not utilize much dialogue in his narrative. In Allen's narrative, he includes many biblical allusions, which increase towards the narrative's end, and these biblical allusions portray Allen's redemption in his narrative because he claims that he should have died. Allen's self-construction is of an American gentleman, and he constructs the narrative on a providential level.[13] Throughout Allen's text, the author tries to establish a self-construction

---

[7] Allen, 45.

[8] Allen, 13–14.

[9] Daniel E. Williams, "Zealous in the Cause of Liberty: Self-Creation and Redemption in the Narrative of Ethan Allen," *Studies in 18th Century Culture* 19 (1990) 337.

[10] Allen, 12; John Clarence Webster, *Sir Brook Watson friend of the Loyalists, first agent of New Brunswick in London* (Sackville: New Brunswick, Mount Allison University, 1924), 13 indicates that Brook Watson of the painting, *Watson and the Shark*, was on The Adamant, and therefore the Watson that Allen describes is the Watson of John Singleton Copley's painting.

[11] Allen, 41.

[12] Allen, 26.

[13] Allen, 26–27.

as an honorable, Yankee gentleman, who is both courageous and brave. For example, when describing Captain Symonds, Allen observes:

> When we were first brought on board, Captain Symonds ordered all the prisoners, and most of the hands on board, to go on the deck, and caused to be read in their hearing, a certain code of laws, or rules for regulation and ordering of their behavior; and then in a sovereign manner, ordered the prisoners, me in particular, off the deck, and never to come on it again; for said he, this is a place for gentlemen to walk[14]

Allen challenges this by walking on the ship's deck in his best attire. In "Zealous in the Cause of Liberty: Self Creation and Redemption in the Narrative of Ethan Allen," Daniel E. Williams claims, "Allen overran the established borders of his life at an early age, and claimed the right to become whatever he wanted to be."[15] This gives the reader an insight to Allen's self-construction because Allen constructs himself as "a full blood Yankee."[16]

Contents of the Narrative

Before becoming a POW, Allen describes a very heroic military life because of the capture of Fort Ticonderoga in 1775. Allen does not mention the help of Benedict Arnold. Allen may have omitted Arnold because Arnold became a traitor in 1779. After his capture of Fort Ticonderoga, Allen led a small group of men northward to Montreal, Quebec. Allen had no commission from the Continental Congress or any colonial government to lead an attack on Montreal. It was here, however, that British troops captured Allen because of miscommunication. Allen does not blame himself or his troops for his captivity, and he remembers his horror as British troops shackle him: ". . . the hand cuff was of a common size and form, but my leg irons (I should imagine) would weigh thirty pounds; the bar was eight feet long, and very substantial . . . The irons were so close upon my ancles, that I could not lie down in any other manner than on my back. . . ."[17] After British forces removed Allen's "shackles" from nearly three years of captivity, Allen visited General Washington at Valley Forge, and later returned home to Vermont. Allen's strong self-construction as a brave, resourceful Yankee explains how he survived the negative and positive treatment that

---

[14] Allen, 17.
[15] Williams, 328.
[16] John Ditsky, "The Yankee Insolence of Ethan Allen," *Canadian Review of American Studies* 1 (1970) 34; Allen, 16.
[17] Allen, 10.

he endured from the British troops.[18] Never defeated by British troops, Allen consistently displayed a strong self-image.

During any type of POW captivity, the prisoner undoubtedly receives very poor treatment, and when writing a personal narrative about the captivity, the author is likely to recall many of the harsh and traumatic details. Allen, however, likes to detail his hardships to make the reader believe that his experience was very harsh when overall it was not. He does this because he receives such harsh treatment from the Tories, not the British. For example, Brook Watson is a nasty bully to Allen through Allen's captivity.[19] After his capture by the British, they board Allen onto a ship called *The Adamant*. While sailing to England to his imprisonment in Pendennis Castle, Allen recalls the rude crew and unsanitary conditions on the ship: "When we asked for water, we were most commonly insulted and derided; and to add to all the horrors of the place, it was so dark that we could not see each other, and were overspread with body lice."[20] Allen notes many instances where the British troops provide him with very poor and bad housing. In one instance that shows how tight and cramped his housing was onboard the vessel to Halifax, Allen writes: "I had now but thirteen [other prisoners] with me of those that were taken in Canada, and remained in goal (with me) in Halifax, who in addition to those that were imprisoned before, made our number about thirty four, who were all locked up in one common large room. . . ."[21] Even as the number of prisoners grew, the British continue to squish them into one room, where the aforementioned unsanitary conditions grew worse. Because of poor housing conditions, many POWs became sick, but Allen only mentions that he was sick once in his entire narrative. His sickness, an ordinary common cold, came prior to a voyage from Pendennis Castle to Ireland. Allen remembers, "Prior to this [the voyage to Ireland] I had taken cold, by which I was in an ill state of health, and did not say much to the officer...,"[22] and further remembers, "I was weak and feeble in consequence of so long and cruel a captivity. . . ."[23] It seems interesting that Allen did not report his sickness to any officers; mostly likely, the officers could have cared less about Allen's health. Continuing to detail the difficulty of his captivity, Allen discusses the possibility that British troops will execute him. Allen often mentions that he

---

[18] Allen, 14.
[19] Allen, 14.
[20] Allen, 13.
[21] Allen, 24.
[22] Allen, 17.
[23] Allen, 22.

is in the hand of an evil nation. At Pendennis Castle, Allen anxiously worries about his "preservation" while the British Parliament discusses his fate. Allen remembers his anxiety at the time:

> But the majority argued, that I ought to be executed, and that the opposition was really a rebellion, but that policy obliged them not to do it, inasmuch as the Congress had then most prisoners in their power: so that my being sent to England for the purpose of being executed, and necessity restraining them, was rather a foil on their laws and authority, and they consequently disapproved of my being sent thither . . . .[24]

Prior to his departure for England, Allen got into a fight with a Tory. Allen recalls that this Tory (not specified) told him that he "…ought to have been executed for his rebellion against New York, and spit in my face. . . ."[25] Allen immediately retaliated by springing up on him and knocking him down. Allen writes, "I challenged him to fight, notwithstanding the impediments that were on my hands, and had the exalted pleasure to see the rascal tremble for fear. . . ."[26]

Although Allen's *Narrative* emphasizes his negative experience as a POW, the text also mentions instances of decent treatment. When imprisoned in either England or Halifax, Allen always received excellent meals: for example, Lieutenant Hamilton, the commander of Pendennis Castle, took great care of Allen with wonderful food. Allen writes, "My personal treatment by Lieutenant Hamilton…was very generous. He sent me every day a fine breakfast and dinner from his own table, and a bottle of good wine."[27] While in Halifax, Allen also notes an excellent meal from a charitable woman named Mrs. Blacden who "…supplied me with a good dinner of fresh meats every day, with garden fruit, and sometimes with a bottle of wine…."[28] Obviously, Allen's treatment is not as bad as he makes it seem because Allen dines on hearty meals numerous times through out the narrative.

Along with excellent nourishment, Allen made excellent friendships, especially with a man named Gilligan, whom he met while sailing to America. Allen thoroughly enjoyed his company, and these two men remained friends until their boat docked in Cape Fear, North Carolina.

---

[24] Allen, 14; Allen claims he learns the details of the debate later.
[25] Allen, 13.
[26] Allen, 13.
[27] Allen, 15.
[28] Allen, 25.

An interesting friendship arose between Allen and an unidentified captor, where both men valued their friendship over a bottle of wine: "That there is greatness of soul for personal friendship to subsist between you and me, as we are upon opposite sides, and may at another day be obliged to face each other in the field."[29] Allen does not describe any friendships with the Loyalists. Lastly, Allen befriends a man named Captain Travis in a prison cell in New York. Allen notes, "I formed an oblique acquaintance with a Capt. Travis, of Virginia, (who was in the dungeon below me) through a little hole which was cut with a penknife, through the floor of my apartment, which communicated with the dungeon. . . ."[30] Allen enjoyed his friendship with Captain Travis, as he writes, "In fine I was charmed with the spirit of the man."[31] Allen's American and British friendships are not the center of his *Narrative*, but British friendships have two effects. Such friendships tend to mute any cruelty of the British, and to make the cruelty of the British more credible by indicating exceptions.

Conclusion

To my reading, the basic plot of *The Narrative of Colonel Ethan Allen* is a survivor narrative, where Allen details the trials and tribulations during his 975-day captivity. This is because Allen visits many different countries and meets many different individuals on both sides of the Atlantic coastline. In the Introduction, Allen states his purpose to write his autobiography, which is out of the sense and duty towards his American country. It also appears that Allen sought to raise support for the Revolution by depicting the brutality he experienced, especially from the Tories. He writes, "Induced by a sense of duty to my county, and by the application of many of my worthy friends, some of whom are of the first characters, I have concluded to publish the following narrative of the extraordinary scenes of my captivity, and the discoveries which I made in the course of the same...."[32] Also, because Allen's narrative is a captivity narrative, he utilized this literary genre of writing as a motive to compile his experience as a POW. Allen wanted to make his conditions sound much worse than they really were. Some POW captives, such as John A. Scott (*Encarnation Prisoners*) and Amos E. Stearns (*Narrative*) tell the author's captivity through the genre of the survivor narrative, but do not seem to augment the severity of the condi-

---

[29] Allen, 27.
[30] Allen, 36.
[31] Allen, 36.
[32] Allen, 1.

Ethan Allen: Colonel Ethan Allen's Captivity

tions they experienced. Like his valiant capture of Fort Ticonderoga, and his brave self-construction in his narrative, Allen wants his autobiography to be a survivor plot with a message to show how to be a patriot survivor in types of POW captivities.

John A. Scott:
Encarnacion Prisoners, 1848

A Mexican-American War Memoir

Logan J. Reed

The Text

ENCARNACION PRISONERS: Comprising an Account of the March of the Kentucky Cavalry from Louisville to the Rio Grande, Together with An Authentic History of the Captivity of the American Prisoners, including Incidents and Sketches of the Men and Things on the Route and in Mexico, was written by John A. Scott in 1848. This text was published by Prentice and Weissinger, as well as by, G. H. Monsarrat & Co's. Steam Press in Louisville, Kentucky. There was no previous record of publication of this narrative prior to 1848. In addition, John A. Scott takes no credit for his authorship on the title page or anywhere else within the text, but notes that the text was written "By a Prisoner."

Encarnacion Prisoners has not been reviewed in detail by any newspaper or magazine to my knowledge. There was no reference to the text in American History and Life for the key words "John A Scott," "Encarnacion Prisoners," or "Prentice and Weissinger Publications."[1] A search of the MLA index for the same key words also yielded no results.[2] In addition, a search of Documenting the South, Making of American, and the *North American Review* failed to yield any information.[3] Based on analysis of the text, *Encarnacion Prisoners* seems to be written for the men who were taken captive in the Mexican-American War, as well as any U.S. citizen who

---

[1] America History and Life searched 3/2/06.
[2] MLA Index searched 3/1/06.
[3] Documenting the South, Making of America, and *North American Review* searched on 3/30/06.

wished to learn about what really took place during the war through the eyes of the POWs. Scott attempts to influence U.S. opinion in favor of the opposition of Santa Anna by showing how close Mexico came to revolution. Considering that the text was published in 1848, this account would have been very relevant to most markets in America.

The Author

John A. Scott was born April 14, 1824 near Richmond, in Jefferson County Ohio. Scott attended district schools prior to moving to Iowa in 1843 to teach. However, he soon returned to the Kentucky-Ohio region where he began to study law and was eventually admitted to the Ohio bar. In the spring of 1846, Scott enlisted as a volunteer member of the Kentucky Cavalry in Mexican-American War. Scott was under the command of Major Gaines in the area between the passage of Encarnacion and San Salvador in Mexico on January 19, 1847 when he became a POW. A Mexican force of three thousand troops overwhelmed their force of slightly under a hundred men. Scott was imprisoned until November 1, 1847, over three hundred days after his original capture. Scott wrote *Encarnacion Prisoners* anonymously in 1848 and had it published in the state of Kentucky. Following his discharge from the military, he stayed in Kentucky where he edited the *Kentucky Whig*, until he moved to Nevada, Iowa in 1856.

Scott remained active personally as well as professionally in Iowa as he engaged in various real estate and farming ventures. In addition, Scott began to become active politically when, in 1859, he was elected to the Iowa State Senate to represent Story, Boone, Hardin, and Hamilton counties. Scott served in the regular sessions in the Senate in 1860, as well as the war time session in 1861. With the dawn of the Civil War, Scott reentered the military with the rank of lieutenant colonel as he "commanded the 32nd Iowa Regiment, 1862–1864."[4] Scott served with such distinction that he rose to the rank of colonel until the end of his service in May 1864.

Following his return to civilian life, Scott was elected Lieutenant-Governor of Iowa as a Republican. Scott, "has been intimately associated with the industrial progress of the State for more than a quarter of a century and has been president of the State Agricultural Society, of the State Road Improvement Association, the Improved Stock Breeders' Association and

---

[4] William Coyle, *Ohio Authors and Their Books. Biographical Data and Selective Bibliographies for Ohio Authors, Native and Resident, 1796–1950* (Cleveland: World, 1962) 558. (John Scott). Email from Reference Desk at Young Library at University of Kentucky 3/9/06 provided a list of biographies that contained information on John A. Scott.

delegate to the National Agricultural Congress."⁵ In 1885, Scott was once again elected to the State Senate where he wrote a bill to establish State Board of Control for various public institutions. After his retirement from public service, Scott wrote a family history, as well as a text entitled, *Story of the Thirty-second Iowa Infantry Volunteers* in 1898.

Framing the Narrative

The copy of the *Encarnacion Prisoners* that was used in this analysis was the Prentice and Weissinger 1848 publication from microfilm made from the copy of the text at the Bancroft Library at the University of California at Berkley. In addition, an original text of the same publication was available at the Beinecke Library at Yale University.⁶ The original copy was very delicate and worn and did not have any type of dusk jacket. The book itself had a gray cover with the title "Encarnacion Prisoners 1848" that appears to be pasted on. The inside cover has a sticker that states, "Yale University- Discover and Settlement of Western America collection of William Robertson," which denotes how the book came to Yale University's possession. The first page has the same title as the cover and there are two blank yellow sheets before and after the text. There are no pictures or maps included in the text. In total, there are only ninety-seven pages of text comprising eight chapters, a conclusion, a list of the men who were captured, seven notes from within the text, and four letters, one each from Major Gaines, Lieutenant Churchill, Captain Heady, and Captain Danley while they were being held in captivity.

Included in the text, there are eight quotations, but Scott does not identify any of the passages with any type of notation or source of authorship. Scott quotes: "From morn till noon, from noon till dewy eve."⁷ This quotation may refer to the travel narrative, *Memoir of an American Lady*.⁸ However, the majority of these quotations do not appear until chapter eight and in the conclusion.

To conclude the narrative, Scott writes, "These are the names of the American prisoners—let them be enrolled upon the tablet of fame!"⁹ This

---

⁵ Benjamin F. Gue, *History of Iowa Vol. IV, 1903*, http://iagenweb.org/civilwar/biographies/biographies.html

⁶ Original text viewed 3/7/06.

⁷ Scott, *Encarnacion Prisoners*, 38.

⁸ Anne M. Grant, *Memoir of an American Lady* (New York, 1836, 1808), 35, Google search 3/23/06.

⁹ Scott, *Encarnacion Prisoners*, 91.

statement gives credit to the men who fought and were captured, as well as identifies whose command each man was under when they were captured. The inclusion of this list shows that the text was meant for the men who were captured at Encarnacion.

Structure of the Narrative

Encarnacion Prisoners is a chronological narrative that follows the Kentucky Cavalry as they receive the call to action in the spring of 1846 in Louisville, Kentucky to enter the Mexican-American War. Scott details that, "after a stupendous march of three months and twenty five-days, and over a tract of near two thousand miles, [the troops] reached the seat of war." [10] Although, the narrative is chronological, it does not focus upon specific dates, but rather upon the event itself, organized as of a travel log, which would have been a popular writing style in the 1840s and 1850s.[11]

A major shift in the mood of the narrative occurs when Scott and the men are taken captive on January 19, 1847. Until the men became POWs, there was a real sense of futility and senselessness in their role in the military. From the point of capture until the release of the POWs, there emerges a sense of importance and pride that is felt throughout the narrative. As the POWs are marched through Mexico, the narrative begins to read like the notes of that of an expedition in which the men are exploring the Mexican terrain and observing the Mexican people.

The major turning point in the narrative occurs following the capture of the men outside Encarnacion. Daniel Drake Henry, a soldier who had been serving as an interpreter for Major Borland, was able to escape by using a mare that Major Gaines had been allowed to keep for himself despite his surrender. This act outraged their Mexican captors and made the soldiers believe that retribution would be soon at hand. Yet, Scott writes, "Major Gaines drew himself up to his full stature, and with a scowl of honest indignation visible in every feature, and smiting himself upon the breast with his hand, said to the enraged Mexican in broad English, 'I am a solider.'"[12] This incident solidified the American's resolve as POWs, as well as showed them that the Mexicans viewed POWs as a commodity, not merely as prisoners.

---

[10] Scott, *Encarnacion Prisoners*, 19.

[11] The travel log style was made famous at the same time by Herman Melville with the works *Omoo* (1847) and *Mardi and a Voyage Thither* (1849).

[12] Scott, *Encarnacion Prisoners*, 37.

John A. Scott: Encarnacion Prisoners

The rest of the narrative details how the men were treated and where they stayed as they were marched around Mexico for roughly the next three hundred days. Scott goes into detail describing the political climate at the time as well as showing how close Mexico was to a revolution of its own due to civil discontent. Scott introduces the major political players and the locations in which these events were transpiring. However, when the men are released from captivity on November 1, 1847, the narrative comes to an abrupt end. There is no mention of anything that took place with the POWs or with the war after the men arrive in New Orleans after a rough one week voyage at sea.

Construction of the Narrative

The style of *Encarnacion Prisoners* is straightforward and not boastful. This may be seen from the beginning of the text as Scott does not even claim authorship of the narrative. At no point in this narrative does Scott refer to himself in the first person and, only after the men become POWs, does he use the term "we" when talking about what is going on. Scott uses quotes at five different instances in the text and does not identify their authors. Through analysis, I have been able to discover that the passage on page 38 from *Memoir of an American Lady,* and the passage on page 39, "so from the lions of this rude animal may spring the proud war-horse that 'smelleth the battle afar off, the thunder of the captain and the shouting, and saith among the trumpets ha! ha! as he goeth on to meet the armed men,'" is from the book of Job 39:25.[13] In addition, the passage on page 79, "None but the brave, none but the brave deserve the fair," is from the English poet and dramatist, John Dryden.[14] Scott's use of quotations reflects his strong educational background since it seems unlikely that an average soldier would probably have been unfamiliar with such passages.

Scott also writes of the beauty as well as dangers of nature that he encounters marching on his way to Mexico and once he is taken captive. "The tarantula is a prodigious black spider, or rather a monster of the spider species—it is as large as a common toad, and can leap the distance of four feet in a single bound."[15] Scott writes this text with such detail that it acts almost as a guidebook for a person who wished to travel. Yet, Scott also takes time to reflect upon the beauty that is all around him. While in captivity he writes, "All over this delightful land of the sun is heard the

---

[13] Scott, *Encarnacion Prisoners*, 39.
[14] Google Search 3/23/06.
[15] Scott, *Encarnacion Prisoners*, 9.

melancholy music of the cooling dove. From the desolate cliff, when far, far below landscapes the most gorgeous and glorious that the eye ever beheld sleep in dozing beauty, the mournful turtle pours forth her softest, sweetest, and saddest strains, as though the goddess of nature delighted to entrance the soul ere she "lapped it in Elysium."[16]

Despite the fact that the men are captive for the majority of the text, surprisingly the captivity is not the central focus of the narrative, but it merely serves as the setting. Scott is very detailed in describing what life was like in the Mexican cities during the Mexican-American War. Scott is very critical of Santa Anna and the mobs of people in the street, referring to them as, "timid slaves and subservient to the will of a despot. . . ."[17] Scott is successful in demonizing the Mexican mobs, but he gives an optimistic look to the future of the country through the capable leadership of M. D. Olaguibal, Governor of Mexico. In describing the man, Scott writes, "He is forty years of age, and enjoys a reputation for honesty and devoted patriotism truly enviable, and is a century at least in advance of the age of the country in which he lives."[18] Despite being held as a POW in Mexico, Scott is not very critical of his captors and recognizes the need for friendly relations with Mexico in the future.

The Contents of the Narrative

John A. Scott enlisted in the army under the command of Major Gaines as a volunteer member of the Kentucky Cavalry. There is a sense of futility in the military activity prior to becoming POW. The march from Louisville to Mexico was brutal and physically exhausting. The men were faced with poor food and water supplies as well as the constant threat of sickness or exhaustion. The situation did not improve when the men reached Mexico as they were called to search towns and guard supply depots.

Scott is very specific in describing how he was taken prisoner. The men were in the town in Encarnacion so that they could find a "point of observation," but were forced to scout out the land. Major Gaines command came across Minon, who was in command of Santa Anna's advance guard. At this point the two commanders agreed to the terms of capitulation. At the time of surrender, the Mexicans made the promise to be fair and to treat the POWs with the honor and dignity. This promise was meet as the men were not subjected to exceptionally harsh treatment, with the

---

[16] Scott, *Encarnacion Prisoners*, 39.
[17] Ibid., 69.
[18] Ibid., 88.

exception of marching, and even allowed to meet with Santa Anna in person, who stated through an interpreter: "that as capricious fortunes of war had thrown them into the hands of the Mexican Government, that they should be treated well; that they would be conducted to the Capital, where he would recommend the, to the highest consideration."[19] The Mexican officers responsible of the safety of the POWs made sure that the men would remain safe because of their value to Mexico in negotiations with the United States.

The Mexican people were a serious threat to the safety of the POWs. In one instance in San Louis Potosi, an angry mob gathered yelling "stone them!" "death to the Yankees!" "kill them!"[20] To provide safety for the POWs Major Romero of Mexico Army ordered the soldiers to clear a path to a convent so the men would be protected. In a similar incident, the POWs were marched into town at night to avoid the Mexican mob. This pattern continued throughout Scott's stay in captivity and only began to subside when the hatred of the Mexican people shifted towards Santa Anna. Towards the end of the war, open rebellion broke out in opposition to Santa Anna in cities such as Vera Cruz.

The other major threat to the safety of the POWs while in captivity was disease. The POWs were subjected in some instances to poor drinking water, long marches, as well as different types of food. Scott notes, "With some Mexicans a dog is luxurious and even a cat is a dainty dish!"[21] It was also not uncommon for the men to be pushed to the brink of exhaustion by having to march forty miles a day in the hot sun. However, if a POW fell ill he had the opportunity to receive proper care. If soldiers fell sick they were sent to the "Sisters of Charity" and if a soldier needed more aid a POW, Major Borland, was a doctor who would provide aid for the POWs despite his refusal to help the Mexican Soldiers.

The POWs were provided with housing based on the rank of the soldier. Officers were given thirty-seven and a half cents per day by the Mexican Government, while the men were only given eighteen and three quarters cents per day. For the most part the POW officers were kept in one room together, separated from their men. Yet, the POWs were given great freedoms such as a woman to cook and wash for them as well as a type of honor system, which allowed the men to venture into town. In fact, the POWs were able to maintain a standard of living above that of the Mexican soldiers who guarded them. Scott noted that the Mexican Ranchero's who

---

[19] Ibid., 46.
[20] Ibid., 49.
[21] Ibid., 54.

guarded the POWs were often treated worse than the POW's themselves. Scott observed that, "The private soldiers in the Mexican service are treated with as much imperiousness and hauteur and even cruelty as the disobedient slaves upon the cotton plantations of the southern part of this Republic."[22] The Ranchero's would steal blankets from the POWs, only to be whipped by the Mexican officers and forced to return the blanket, only to repeat the process over again.

The POWs were able to experience great freedoms while they were being held in the Mexican cities. Some men chose to attend the theater, while others took an interest in the Mexican women. Scott wrote that while in Toluca, "The Mexican ladies had been captivated by Yankee heroism, and were delighted with the attentions of the prisoners when incidentally paid, but feared to associate with them lest they might be considered traitorous to their country."[23] Scott is very critical of the Mexican people as well as their culture. In fact, Scott goes as far as to state: "Mexicans have no confidence in each other, not in any body, nor thing."[24] Scott and the other POWs witnessed the resentment of the Mexican people towards their government.

With an American victory looming, the POWs were very worried about what might happen to them before their release. General Scott was able to push Santa Anna back and this created fear throughout the Mexican people as well as the POWs. Scott wrote: "Nor had we forgotten the historic fact that as soon as the Spaniards gained the advantage during the Peninsular war, the French Prisoners were dragged from, their dungeons, paraded in triumph and put to death."[25] The Americans were well aware of the history of the treatment of POWs from past wars in Mexico and were very cautious. Nevertheless, Scott notes that the greatest threat posed to them came from the Mexican people, not the army. As the communications between of the Mexican Government and local governments continued to erode, what was to happen with the POWs remained a question of debate. Matters were only complicated when word came back that: "They insisted that General Scott had violated the laws of nations and executed men who had the right to be treated as prisoners of war; and now they were justified should they retaliate and wreak vengeance upon the American Prisoners."[26] Nevertheless, the importance of the American POWs to Mexico was not

---

[22] Ibid., 49.
[23] Ibid., 79.
[24] Ibid., 67.
[25] Ibid., 63.
[26] Ibid., 85.

jeopardized by the actions of General Scott. Through the help of the Governor of Mexico, M. D. Olaguibal, the POWs were able to remain safe and obtain their release on November 1, 1847, some three hundred days after their original capture.

Conclusion

Encarnacion Prisoners is an adventure narrative, which follows the major events of the Mexican-American War and details what life was like as a POW. Scott goes into great detail in describing the beauty and grandeur of the land to allow the reader to get a feel for what the men experienced. It is clear that he did not write this narrative as a means for self-aggrandizement but to show the resolve with which the volunteer Kentucky Cavalry served with despite their capture. This sentiment is clearly shown by Scott's decision to never refer to himself in the first person. Moreover, this shows the bond that existed amongst the men as well as to show that their captivity did not supercede the war effort.

Although in some instances, Scott succeeds in demonizing the Mexican people, he dedicates the majority of the narrative to looking upon the situation of the Mexican government. Scott is convinced that through the leadership of the opposition to Santa Anna that Mexico will be able to achieve prosperity in their beautiful land.

The narrative may be broken up into three parts: first the march of the Kentucky Cavalry to Mexico, secondly the capture and captivity of the American Soldiers, and finally the negotiations to achieve the release of the POWs. This narrative is a unique window into the lives of the soldiers because it shows that the American POWs were treated with more honor and dignity than most of the Mexican soldiers.

Belle Boyd:
Belle Boyd in Camp and Prison

A Civil War Memoir

THOMAS KETTMER

The Text

BELLE BOYD in Camp and Prison, written by Maria "Belle" Boyd, was originally published in 1865.[1] For the purpose of this examination, I used a reprint published by the Louisiana State University Press in 1998.[2] Although I am sure Boyd enjoyed the fame and notoriety that came along with being a female spy, her motive and reason for writing a memoir was simple—she needed the money. She wrote in an effort to provide for herself and her daughter after the death of her husband.[3] Moreover, she makes an attempt to draw in not only the northerners as readers, but also attempts to captivate and draw in the English readers as well.[4]

The memoir seems ironic in several ways. Although the memoir describes Boyd's involvement in the American Civil War, it was written while Boyd was in London, England. Boyd's narrative ends abruptly in chapter twenty one when she marries Samuel Hardinge, and, with the exception of

---

[1] There were two editions: the English edition (London: Saunders, Otley and Co., 1865) in two volumes; and the American edition (New York: Blelock & Company, 1865) in one volume. Both contained a journal written by Lt. Hardinge, Boyd's husband.

[2] Belle Boyd in Camp and Prison, with a forward by Drew Gilpin Faust, and an introduction by Sharon Kennedy Nolle (Baton Rouge: Louisiana, 1998), hereafter cited as Boyd.

[3] Lyde Cullen Sizer, "Belle Boyd," in American National Biography, eds. John A. Garraty and Mark C. Carnes, 24 vols. (New York Oxford University Press, 1999), 3:308–9.

[4] Some features directed at northern readers include: the final chapter on Lincoln, and some favorable descriptions of Union officers (e.g., Boyd, 108, 113, 120, 131). The narrative begins with an address to English readers, and contains several references that might charm British readers, for example, Boyd, 69, 71, 75, 80, 105, 134, 149, 181, 198, 204, 247, 266.

a final chapter on Lincoln's assassination, the remainder of the text is taken from Hardinge's journal. Hardinge's authorship is not reflected on the title page. Boyd, an interesting and unique figure, has been the subject of a number of books and articles.[5]

The Author

Maria Isabella Boyd was born on May 4, 1844 in what is now present-day Martinsburg, West Virginia.[6] She attended the Mount Washington Female College of Baltimore, a prestigious school at the time. She came from a close, tight knit family that had some power and influence in the region which she lived. Boyd's father, Benjamin, joined the second Virginia Infantry in 1861 and as a result, she became intrigued with the war. When Union and Confederate forces fought around the area of Martinsburg and Northern soldiers invaded Boyd's home to erect the Union Flag on July 4, she took a pistol and killed one of them after he insulted Boyd and her mother.[7] She gave her side of the account by saying, "…one of the soldiers, thrusting himself forward, addressed my mother and myself in language as offensive as it is possible to conceive. I could stand it no longer; my indignation was roused beyond control; my blood was literally boiling in my veins; I drew out my pistol and shot him. He was carried away and mortally wounded, and soon after expired."[8] Because of her staunch support of the Confederacy she was interned like a POW on three occasions.[9]

Because of her efforts and contributions to the Confederacy, Boyd claims she was honored by Stonewall Jackson, who made her a captain and honorary aide-de-camp on his staff. After escaping to England, Boyd married Samuel Hardinge, a Union officer who had been in charge of her captivity. Boyd wrote her memoir in England after the death of her husband

---

[5] When searching online databases, I found the following: 8 hits on America History and Life; 28 hits for "Belle Boyd" but 0 results for a review of the memoir in the Historical *New York Times*; and only 1 result on the MLA Index.

[6] The following sources were consulted for Boyd's life: Sizer, "Boyd" (cited above); the introductions by Faust and Noelle; Louis A. Sigaud: *Belle Boyd Confederate Spy* (Richmond: Dietz Press, 1944).

[7] She insists that the Yankee solder got what he deserved and she had "done perfectly right," Boyd, 83.

[8] According to her memoir there was an investigation, but she was not punished although a guard was sent to her house for "protection purposes," Boyd, 82.

[9] The Baltimore Jail, 1862 (about seven days); Old Capitol Prison, 1862 (about 30 days); Carroll Prison (about 90 days), and Boyd was put under a sort of "cabin" arrest after the ship on which she was sailing to Bermuda was captured by Union forces.

and the birth of her daughter while recovering from typhoid.[10] Once she returned in the United States, she started performing and acting all over the country. She died on June 11, 1900 in Wisconsin. Belle Boyd was a very audacious woman.

Framing of the Narrative

Though she obviously favored the Southern Confederacy, the original copy of Boyd's memoir had the Union and Confederate flags intertwined over an anchor on the cover.[11] Following a photographic reproduction of Boyd, there is a preface from Boyd's publisher, George Augusta Sala who begins by noting how Boyd came up to him and said "Will you take my life?" This sounds like an odd question, but Boyd was not asking to be killed, but rather was proposing that Sala take her life story and read over what she recounted from memory about all of her past experiences during wartime in America. Sala goes on to admit that Boyd was desperate for money and had a sense of despair about her because of the imprisonment and death of her husband. Sala refers to Boyd, by her married name, Madame Hardinge.[12]

Chapters 22 to 27 were written not by Belle Boyd, but rather by her first husband, the late Samuel L. Hardinge. There are 53 pages in total written by Hardinge that Boyd incorporated into her memoir. It almost seems as if the audacious Boyd looses her voice when she marries, however, the six chapters by Hardinge, except for the absence of quotations of poetry, are similar in style to the chapters written by Boyd, and they contain the description of the worst behavior toward POWs by Union captors.[13]

Boyd's memoir contains some twenty quotations of poetry. The most frequently quoted poet is Byron followed by Virgil, several English and some American poets.[14] In some cases Boyd adapts the lines she quotes

[10] Another irony is that she married three times and two of these men fought for the Union. In chapter one, she even says "a true woman always loves a real soldier" (Boyd, 77).

[11] The anchor seems to have wreathlike decoration. It was not possible to investigate the symbolism of this art work. I assume the art work represents a strategy to reach both a northern and southern audience.

[12] Boyd, 55–56. The introduction by Sala is noted on the title pages of both the London and New York editions, but the phrase, "A Friend of the South," is omitted from the New York edition.

[13] Both Boyd and Hardinge employ a lot of dialogue some of which is in dialect, for example: Boyd, 82, 104, 114, 117, 198; Hardinge, 213, 216, 250, and both use the word, "Bastille" to describe Union prisons.

[14] Poetry is quoted in Boyd as follows: Byron, 70, 78, 136, 193; Virgil, 168, 184; Boyd, 135, 198 (possibly derived from Virgil's *Georgics*); Thomas Moore, 74; Bayard Taylor, 90; Horace Walpole, 130; Richard Lovelace, 134; Sir Walter Scott, 158; Percy Shelley, 175;

to fit better with the situation she is describing, and in two instances the poetry is either by Boyd or has been modified to the point that it is hard to trace. Boyd alludes to the *Bible* on several occasions; twice to Edger Allen Poe's "The Raven," and once to James Fenimore Cooper's *The Spy*, a text from which she seems to have learned some techniques of spying.[15] There are two excerpts from newspaper articles, one in English and one in French, describing Boyd's wedding, and occasional references to coverage of Boyd in newspapers.[16]

Boyd concludes her memoir with a reflection about the assassination of Abraham Lincoln that she claims was added after her memoir was written. Boyd notes that in spite of her political differences with the President she "… had no animosity against the honorable gentleman who has wielded the scepter of Northern power for four long years…," but her main point in this added chapter is that the South had nothing to do with Lincoln's assassination. She addresses her English audience one last time by saying "Englishmen! I appeal to your impartial judgment…," and she concludes by challenging those who warned her not to publish the memoir with a typically dramatic declaration, "I will not recede."[17]

Structure of the Narrative

Belle Boyd in Camp and Prison begins with a short four page first chapter in which Boyd warns readers that she has to rely on her memory for the account because she did not write her experiences down on paper. Since she is writing this from London, Boyd warns her British audience that she must reminisce and recount her times growing up in the war torn Southern lands of America.[18] The short chapters do not have titles but instead are designated by Roman numerals.[19]

The narrative is chronological, but there are a couple of instances where Boyd digresses from the story and then goes back to telling the story. This can be seen on page 77 where in the middle of the page she says "to

Vincenzo Monti, 171; Shakespeare, 191; James T. Fields, 206; Robert Southey, 206.

[15] Some Bible allusions include: Luke 17:27, 72; Genesis 8:6, 88; 1 Kings 18:45, 136; Poe, 122, 128; Cooper, 101.

[16] Boyd, 207–9; Boyd explains that hostile press coverage resulted from a clash with a reporter (Boyd, 112).

[17] Boyd, 264–65.

[18] There was an article in the *Martinsburg Journal* in 1992 saying "Was Belle Boyd a liar? It goes to show how even some people in her hometown 100 years later question the validity and accuracy of her statements."

[19] There are 27 chapters; the longest, chapter, twelve, is fourteen pages.

return from this digression" and then returns to the story. Also there is a lot of dialogue and discussions that occur in the memoir.[20] For example, she recounts the conversation with one of her "maids,"[21] who informs her that the Union soldiers have intentions to burn down her home. Although it seems unlikely that Boyd would remember exactly what her servant told her, she does her best impression and even writes in a tone that may reflect a slave's way of speaking.[22]

Construction of the Narrative

Belle Boyd in Camp and Prison is constructed to illustrate Boyd's daring heroism and her lady-like femininity through the metaphor of domesticity invaded. The metaphor of domesticity invaded is more or less sustained throughout the memoir and it serves as a way of reconciling Boyd's audacious manly behavior and her persona as a southern lady.

Boyd is thrust into a soldier's role when Yankees invade her home in Martinsburg. Stonewall Jackson, who is described as both a father figure and a great hero, serves to validate Boyd's roles. For example, a letter from Jackson is quoted to substantiate Boyd's claim that her unladylike audacity has helped the South: "I thank you, for myself and for the army, for the immense service that you have rendered your country today. Hastily, I am your friend."[23] During her three imprisonments Boyd's gentility almost always compels respectful treatment from her captors.

Her marriage is constructed as a decisive return to a domestic role. Immediately preceding the two long newspaper accounts of the marriage Boyd notes that she made a report to the Confederate States Commissioner in England that "…terminated Belle Boyd's connection with the Southern Government for the time being."[24] Her appearance as an author, like her appearance in camp and prison, is presented as the result of another invasion of her domesticity—the death of her husband.

---

[20] This can be seen on pages 82, 104, 117, 191.

[21] She refers to the help she receives as "servants" or "negro maids," and makes a point of never referring to the help as slaves because they could justify it this way.

[22] For example the slave says "massa" as opposed to master when probably referring back to Belle's father, Benjamin. Boyd also imitates Yankee intonation 'cute for acute (Boyd, 200), footnote 13 above gives other examples.

[23] Boyd, 110.

[24] Ibid., 206.

Contents of the Narrative

Boyd begins by telling about her early home and family life and how the Civil War intrudes into her life starting with the enlisting of her father in the Confederate Army. In the first chapter, Boyd writes about growing up in a family where she was loved by a caring father and mother and what it was like to live in a part of the country where battles of war would take place. She compares Washington, D.C. to the city of Paris during its turbulent, revolutionary times during the late 1700s.

Much of the narrative revolves around her being arrested and exiled numerous times. She claims that after being summoned by the Yankee Army, she was not frightened. Instead she "…felt the spirit of the Douglas, from whom I descended." This is a reference to her lineage and established family past. From then on, Boyd notes "…I was a suspect." Boyd explains early on in the account that because she was suspect "…all the mischief done to the Federal Cause was laid…" and charged to her.[25]

Belle Boyd definitely was intelligent and had enough street smarts to know how to become a successful spy for the Confederacy. One of her main duties was to inform Confederate officers of the Union's movements. She did this by giving information to Turner Ashby, a colonel in the Confederate Army. As a result of her diligent and good work, she was became a courier general for Stonewall Jackson and Beauregard.[26]

She easily can be seen as a woman who was sly, crafty and even deceitful. The fact that she was able to eavesdrop and overhear conversations of important Union military officers without being caught shows her aptitude for espionage. Even though she was caught a handful of times and eventually banished to Canada, she still was able to help her side in the war. Nevertheless, Boyd claims to be an "impartial historian" and she maintains "I will not shrink from the truth when it is unfavorable to my countrymen."[27]

In the summer of 1862, Boyd was detained at the Eutaw House, which was located in Baltimore, Maryland. Boyd recounts how she was able to display a small Confederate flag while under guard on the trip to Baltimore. After initial annoyance, Boyd recalls the guards thought it "…an excellent joke that a convoy of Confederate prisoners should be brought in

---

[25] Ibid., 84.

[26] It is said she ran across a field with exploding gunfire just to give a report to General Jackson. As a result, the Confederates gained a victory at the Battle of Front Royal. This is described in the intro on page 6, 7.

[27] Ibid., 189.

under a Confederate flag." Boyd only stayed at the Eutaw House one week and then was sent home back to Martinsburg[28].

In March of 1863, Belle Boyd was arrested under orders of Secretary Stanton and taken to the Old Capitol Prison.[29] She was presented with a copy of rules and regulations indicating that she would "be punished by having her door locked" if she communicated with any of the other prisoners. Considering the circumstances, her internment does not seem too bad. She was able to pack a trunk with her own personal belongings. At various points throughout the memoir, she is able to trump "Yankee meanness" by displaying her gentile Southern charm. This is shown one time when it came to food and that she would be usually served the following items: soup, beef steak, chicken, boiled corn, tomatoes, Irish stew, potatoes, bread and butter, cantaloupes, peaches, pears , and grapes. Boyd admits that on her first night in prison could "be painted in dark colors," however, at night time she "watched, thought, and prayed."[30] Things went from bad to worse when her thumb was broken by one of the guards at the prison and Boyd started to cry because of the pain.[31]

In August of 1863, Boyd was taken again to prison in Washington D.C., however this time it was to the Carroll Prison, a former hotel. She describes the Carroll Prison as a "receptacle for rebels, prisoners of state, hostages, blockade-runners, smugglers, desperadoes, spies, criminals under sentence of death, and lastly a large number of Federal officers convicted of defrauding the Government."[32] Boyd admits that in prison she was greatly relived after meeting her "neighbors" because they too were Southern sympathizers. One good part of her experience in Carroll Prison was that she received permission to walk around the Capitol Square at night time to get fresh air. Sadly, however, Secretary Stanton found out and he revoked this "parole." Stanton is constantly portrayed as a Yankee ogre.

Boyd describes many bad things that happen to her or to loved ones that seem unfair because they are out of her control. She implies that the source of many negative remarks about her in newspapers resulted from her

---

[28] She explains that she was "placed under a strict surveillance and forbidden to leave the town," (Ibid., 95).

[29] The letter from Sec. Stanton read: "Sir: You will proceed immediately to Front Royal, Virginia, and arrest if found there, Miss Belle Boyd, and bring her at once to Washington. I am respectfully your obedient servant, E.M. Stanton."

[30] Her feelings and recount of the first night are on page 136.

[31] Ibid., 141.

[32] Ibid., 155; Boyd notes that newspapers described President Lincoln as "Napoleonic" in his punishment of them for their misdeeds.

rejection of the advances of a reporter for the *New York Herald*. As a result of her rebuffs, he never forgave her and he became "an inveterate enemy."[33] Another tribulation that affected Boyd is found in Hardinage's journal. While she was always "respected" and treated well by the enemy, her husband suffered the opposite. He recounts in his own personal journal that he was attacked violently by Other POWs who chanted "Toss him! Toss the swell cove! mash him! Jam him!" Also, Mr. Hardinage describes a type of water torture that would be used to mess with the inmates.[34]

Conclusion

Belle Boyd in Camp and Prison is unique among the POW memoirs considered in this study in three ways: the memoir has a dual authorship (Boyd and Hardinge), Boyd was a spy rather than a soldier or privateer, and Boyd's home in Virginia was invaded and occupied by the enemy. Boyd's presentation of her self leaves this reader wondering if Boyd in the process of constructing a persona that is appealing, in spite of the many boundaries it trespasses, is describing her past or presenting a model for the future. The Union victory and post-war period of Reconstruction, when the enemy would be present in the South more than ever, would make every southern woman's home occupied territory, and call for more audacious Southern ladies like Boyd. In many ways *Belle Boyd in Camp and Prison* is like the etymology Boyd provides for "skedaddle," a word which was first used during the Civil War. Boyd claims a Greek verb, *skedao*, is the origin of skedaddle. Her etymology is elegant and possible, but more likely improbable and fanciful, and yet Boyd's attempt to give a classical origin to a Civil War word conveys a certain charming insightfulness into how humans can construct history as her memoir illustrates how humans can construct the experience of defeat and internment.[35]

---

[33] This is found in the beginning of chapter 6.

[34] Boyd, 220; Hardinge describes how a prisoner would be "fastened in an immovable position beneath a faucet that permitted to escape, every second, one drop of water, which fell always in one spot upon the forehead, producing a most fearful torture, resulting eventually in insanity" (Ibid., 218).

[35] Boyd, 105, footnote. The author acknowledges the assistance of Fr. Thomas McCreesh in looking up the Greek verb. There is a museum today located in Boyd's hometown of Martinsburg, West Virginia that shows ten displays rooms and gives facts and details about her life. It is called "The Belle Boyd House" and is located at her childhood home in Martinsburg, West Virginia. A website which has information about the museum and can be seen at http://www.bchs.org/civilwar.html.

Solon Hyde:
A Captive of War

A Civil War Memoir

EMILY ROACH

The Text

A *CAPTIVE OF War* was originally published in 1900 by the McClure, Philips and Co., a quality commercial publisher.[1] No reviews were found for this memoir but one book notice was found using a Google search in the National Museum of Civil War Medicine online Store.[2] It was a short piece explaining briefly what Solon Hyde recalls in his account of his time in POW camps of the Civil War. There were no references to this text in the MLA Index or in America History and Life.[3] After reading this text it appears the intended audience was general readers interested in Civil War POW survivor stories. The title of Hyde's memoir connects his captivity with war and not with a specific internment camp or with the forces that held him. Although this choice of wording in the title could reflect the fact that Hyde was interned in several camps, it may also indicate that Hyde thought that his experiences were determined more by the fortunes of war than by the particular circumstances in which he found himself or the particular personalities he encountered. Hyde's memoir was published thirty-five years after he experienced the events it describes; when Hyde wrote the memoir is not known.

---

[1] McClure, Phillips and Co, hereafter cited as Hyde. In 1996 *A Captive of War* with supplemental materials was published by the Burd Street Press, Shippensburg Pennsylvania. In the reprint there is a preface (x–xi) written by Neil Thompson a great-grandson of Solon Hyde. *A Captive of War* does not seem to have been serialized before it was printed by McClure, Philips and Co, but it was possible to check only the Making of America journals on line.

[2] Google Search, 4/29/06; no review could be found using the Historical New York Times.

[3] MLA Index and America History and Life searched 4/28/06.

Emily Roach

The Author

Solon Hyde (1838–1920) grew up in Rushville, Ohio.[4] He was the son of Dr. Simon Hyde and Anne Coulson. In 1861, when Hyde was twenty-two, he enlisted himself into Company K of the 17th Ohio Volunteer Infantry. When he joined he was a hospital steward. He was captured in Georgia at the Battle of Chickamauga and taken into the Libby and Pemberton prisons. Then he moved to Danville where he briefly escaped, after a few thwarted attempts. He was then recaptured and sent to the Andersonville prison where he stayed for a six-month period. After Andersonville he went to his last prison in Salisbury, North Carolina and his time as a POW ended in 1865. Hyde spent 17 months (September 20, 1863–February 27, 1865), roughly 510 days as a captured soldier in these camps. He left the service one month after repatriation, and on March 18, 1865 he married his beloved fiancée, Czarina. Together they had eight children. After the Civil War ended Hyde helped Clara Barton to identify the bodies at Andersonville. Later in his life Hyde moved to Indiana and Missouri where he was involved in various businesses. He retired to California, but it had not been possible to establish where Hyde was living when his memoir was published. Hyde dedicated his memoir as a tribute of appreciation to Miss Clara Barton. This is the only known work written by the author.[5]

Framing the Narrative

A Captive of War Memoir does not have any photographs on the cover or inside. The cover has a drawing of what appears to be two soldiers standing in front of a wrought iron gate, or possibly a jail cell. What exactly the artwork on the cover represents is not explained inside of the book either.[6]

---

[4] Biographical information on Hyde is drawn from the preface to the 1996 edition.

[5] It was not possible to search for an obituary for Hyde in the *Los Angeles Times*, but it was possible to confirm that Hyde was buried in the Inglewood Cemetery, Inglewood California through a Civil War Veterans' site.

[6] Solon Hyde, *A Captive of War* (New York: McClure, Phillips and Co., 1900). The existence of a simple dust cover is confirmed by an email from Owen D. Kubik, Kubik Fine Books Ltd. The cover of the 1996 edition is much different. There are three photographs overlapping one another taken from The Photographic History of the Civil War depicting the issuing rations in Andersonville Prison, August 1864, the Corner of Libby Where Federal Officers Tunneled Under the Street, and Burying the Dead at Andersonville, Summer of 1864 the three photographs were all © 1911, Review of Reviews Co. There is also a photograph of Hyde unnumbered page ii. There are no dates or captions to indicate where the picture was taken, during what year and whether or not it was before, after or during Solon Hyde's capture.

The book is dedicated to Miss Clara Barton "Whose Life Work Has been to minister to the bettering Of the Condition of the unfortunate in *War, Pestilence and Famine,* This book is respectfully inscribed as a tribute of appreciation By the Author, *Columbus, Ohio*".[7] There is some quoted matter inside the memoir which would indicate that Hyde utilized some outside sources for this work and not only his own personal information.[8] Hyde included some allusions and a few quotations in his memoir to enhance his own ideas. He referred to the writings of Petroleum V. Nasby, Mark Twain and Robert Burns, a speech of Jefferson Davis and a remark of Madame Roland, and to the Bible.[9] The memoir contains extensive direct dialogue, and one can assume that these quotes were paraphrased because one can assume Hyde did not have a log during his time as a POW in which he kept track of every conversation he had during his time there.[10] Although Hyde is not a famous author and he did not create any other known works, he did cleverly title each chapter of his memoir describing a different event or day during his time as a POW.

Structure of the Narrative

A Captive of War Memoir begins with the Battle of Chickamauga where Hyde was first captured as a POW on the second day, September 19, 1863. The narrative is basically chronological and describes the events and days of captivity as they pass. For the most part he does not stray backwards or forwards in his story but tells the story as he experienced it day by day. The memoir is mainly a single constructed perspective. It does not use a stream of consciousness or speak in the third person. He does not begin by describing his life before the army, and he does not conclude by describing his life afterwards. Since the narrative is written sequentially, a definite turning point is not apparent.[11] The narrative ends with Hyde's march back into the freedom. It does not end with much of a resolution only that he is finally free after his 510 day sentence as a prisoner. His conclusion just briefly touches on how elated he was to finally escape imprisonment. The

---

[7] Hyde, 5.

[8] Hyde remarks, "But I am getting ahead of my diary . . . ," a remark that implies *A Captive of War* was based on earlier writings (Ibid., 123).

[9] Hyde: Nasby, 46; Twain, 298; Burns, 55; Davis, 321–24; Roland, 389; Bible, 56, 175. There is a quotation on page 357 that could not be identified.

[10] Ibid., 25, 27, 36–37; 79–81, 16, 132–36, 155–57, 200–210, 238–44, 279–88, 338–39.

[11] Hyde's description of his transfer to in the hospital dispensary at Andersonville could be read as life saving event and, therefore, a turning point, but Hyde calls his transfer the result of chance, Ibid., 242–44.

only resolution was his unabashed excitement to finally be let back into the real world and a prisoner no more: "To be free again and to feel that we were breathing the air of freedom was enough."[12]

Construction of the Narrative

In Hyde's writing there does not seem to be any consistent style of writing. However there are a few instances where he used a burlesque style. For example, he uses the word, "skedaddle" in an amusing description of the rapid departure of the Union medical personnel.[13] Hyde gives a comical account of a Roman Catholic chaplain who hated anything "secesh."[14] Hyde's description of the "sugar riot," a dispute that arose among the POWs at Pemberton Prison over how to divide sugar that was pilfered from the basement, is wry, perhaps even picaresque.[15] In one startling instant Hyde addresses the reader a rhetorical move that seems very uncharacteristic as far as the rest of his writing is concerned. Here, Hyde asks, "But, I ask any candid man, was it right that Wirz should hang and they go free."[16] Hyde is asking his audience, in the form of a rhetorical question, if they think is right to execute only the commander at Andersonville when he was not responsible for planning the internment camp or for the end of POW exchanges. This is the only instance where Hyde addresses readers with a question.

Hyde also uses metaphors but very sparingly. He compares the Confederates trying to get away from Columbia, South Carolina with the swells of the ocean. "As the long line of scum indicates the approach of the tidal swell, so this anxious hurrying away from Columbia indicated the near approach of a power as irresistible in its course s the waves of the sea."[17] The other scene where Hyde uses metaphors is on the last page of his memoir where he describes seeing the Union flag at his repatriation: "It was the emblem of Life, of Light, of Home, and was rendered doubly dear to us by our long sojourn beneath the shadow of one whose reign was Terror!"[18]

To my reading *A Captive of War Memoir* is basically a survivor account that narrates the sequence of events during Hyde's internment and attributes the events that Hyde experiences more to chance or to the fortunes

---

[12] Ibid., 388.
[13] Ibid., 24.
[14] Ibid., 60, "secesh" means secessionist.
[15] Ibid., 84–87.
[16] Ibid., 189.
[17] Ibid., 354.
[18] Ibid., 389.

of war than to his individual agency or that of his captors.[19] The occasional ironic, even picaresque tone, employed in describing certain episodes is well adapted to a survivor's story that seeks to avoid blaming the adversities the author experiences on demonic enemies and Hyde's memoir contains numerous descriptions of the decent and charitable behavior of individual Confederates.[20] But the Confederacy is frequently described in the most negative terms. Hyde maintains that the Confederate mistreatment of POWs was intentional, and he attributes this inhumanity to something diabolical about the Confederacy.[21] Sometimes Hyde's negative description of the Confederacy is quite explicit as when he describes the spire of a Richmond church, " . . . we knew that, though it pointed silently heavenward, its foundation was laid in a place akin to hell," but his more characteristic approach is to reveal the character of the Confederacy through what he presents as the candid remarks of Southerners.[22] The monologue of a Charleston gentleman who explains that secession was intended to advance Southern aristocracy, and Hyde's implausible dialogues with an attaché about General Butler and with Mr. Richwine about how to protect Richwine's capital in slaves are examples of how in the course of telling his story Hyde conveys to his readers his opinion of the character of the Confederacy.[23] In a memoir which reads like a survivor's story Hyde has constructed a critique of the Confederacy that may be all the more telling because of its indirectness.[24]

Contents of the Narrative

Hyde did not describe much else beside his time as a prisoner. His story begins with the Battle of Chickamauga in Georgia where he fatefully was captured and it ends seventeen months later when he was finally released once again. Hyde did not explain much about his military service before he was captured. Hyde spent roughly 510 days (seventeen months) as a

---

[19] The most serious injury Hyde describes results from the accidental discharge of a "gun" (Ibid., 386).

[20] Hyde: 27–29 (Col. Scott), 70 (woman), 89 (physicians), 118 (Dr. Dance), 140 (Dr. Hunter), 175 (old woman), 327–28 (Wirtz gives Hyde a pass), 359–60 (soldier), 374–80 (Richwine), 382–83 (Noles).

[21] Hyde: 71 (the selection of bullies for guards), 121 (Andersonville), 388 (Confederate prison plans), 57, 67, 333 (Southern inhumanity and diabolism).

[22] Ibid., 99.

[23] Ibid., 43–46, 132–35, 375–79. Chapter 44 on John C. Calhoun is very explicit.

[24] Hyde also criticizes Northern Democrats and Union policies but in more moderate terms, for example, Ibid., 53, 237, 266–68.

POW dating from September 20, 1863 to February 27, 1865. He was interned in five prisons: Libby, Pemberton, Danville, Andersonville and Salisbury. Hyde vividly describes the malnutrition he experienced and the resulting scurvy and other illnesses from which he nearly died.[25] He recalls sucking the joints and tendons off of bones to try and get a little more to eat.[26] A great portion of the memoir describes his efforts to survive. The general description of Hyde's POW experience is hellish because there were so many problems with the food, housing, medical care, punishment, and oppressive prison guards. Overall Hyde described his feelings as depressed, despairing and numb as if reduced to a lower state.

Hyde describes numerous friendly relationships with other POWs and some Southerners. In two cases his friendships with POWs at Andersonville, Felix and Schroeder, seem to be responsible for his survival. Felix provides a place for Hyde to sleep and he introduces him various survival tactics. Schroeder recommends Hyde for an opening in the Andersonville pharmacy, and Hyde's transfer outside the stockade enables him to eat food that checks the fatal advance of scurvy.[27]

Hyde mentions some adventures during his POW experience. His escape from Danville provides interesting descriptions of the country, the characters he encountered. The trial and execution of the "raiders" at Andersonville, and the POW police force that sprang up to keep the camp under control is characterized as ". . . the most thrilling episode of internal dissention occurring during the history of prison life."[28]

Conclusion

The main objective of Solon Hyde's memoir seems to be the simple fact that he wanted to tell a story. Hyde was clearly very affected by what happened during his time as a POW and felt it was necessary to share with a large audience exactly what happened and how it affected his life during and also afterwards. The plot seems to be based on how and when he was captured, his torturous life during captivity and his final release. The fact that he does not explain much about his life before his capture or after his release seems to be a clear indication of what his intent was. He wanted those who read his memoir to understand his ordeal and how it affected him and so many other Union soldiers like him. Hyde was tortured, shot

---

[25] Hyde carried the scars from scurvy on the bones in his legs for the rest of his life.
[26] Hyde, 77.
[27] Ibid., 209, 244.
[28] Ibid., 224.

at, fell victim to disease and still maintained the courage and bravery to help his fellow Union brethren as a hospital steward. He wrote this to convey to others what he went through, how difficult it was and how he was able to overcome for the love of his country. Hyde wanted people to know about his tragic ordeal and how he overcame great adversity, and he also wanted to inform his readers about the Confederacy as he saw it.

Dr. John H. King:
Three Hundred Days in a Yankee Prison

A Civil War Memoir

CHRISTOPHER EMMENS

The Text

THREE HUNDRED *Days in a Yankee Prison*, written by Dr. John H. King was published by JAS P. Davis, Atlanta, Georgia in 1904.[1] King's POW account, published in a one-volume work approximately 48 years after his POW experience, is one hundred and fourteen pages in length with a preface written by the author. King's motive for writing was to present ". . . a truthful account of his capture, imprisonment, and sufferings in a Federal prison [to] . . . those who still harp on the 'cruelties of Andersonville. . . ."[2] No reviews or examinations of this text have been found.[3]

---

[1] The Library of Congress copy available on line as a link from the LC catalog entry for the book was used for this study: (http://lcweb2.loc.gov/cgi-bin/ampage?collId=gdc3&fileName=scd0001_20001109004thpage.db), hereafter cited as King. There is also 1959 reprint (Kennesaw, GA: Continental, 1959). Both printings contain several apparent printer's errors, for example, 75, "which" for "with," 77, "Wyath" for "Wyeth," 83, "eneny" for "enemy," 92 "thing" for "think."

[2] King, 12; Because King mentions one Confederate POW account published in *The Century Magazine* (King, 77), it is possible that King read the series of POW memoirs *The Century Magazine* published between 1889 and 1891. For a description of this series see Ann Fabian, *The Unvarnished Truth: Personal Narratives in Nineteenth-Century America* (Berkeley: University of California Press, 2000), 122–23.

[3] Sources used were: *The Atlanta Journal Constitution* online archives, the *Historical New York Times*, the *Book Review Digest*, the *MLA Index*, and America History and Life.

51

The Author

Dr. John H. King was born in 1843.[4] Before the Civil War, King lived on a small plantation or farm. His family had some servants and slaves, but King does not describe the family as very wealthy. He grew up in Georgia with three other brothers along with his father. King does not mention going to school before the war, but he does explain that he joined the army mainly because his fellow Georgians were also going to war.[5] King enlisted as a Private in the Confederate Army, he later became a surgeon after the war and worked in a Confederate Soldiers Home in Atlanta.[6]

Framing of the Narrative

There is a preface to the book, and no dust jacket that could be found. There is also a photograph of King in the beginning, but no dedication until page 114. King dedicates his work to the women of the South. At the beginning of each chapter there is a title, and under the title the main events of the chapter are listed. There are several quotes made in the text by King. On page 94 there is a quote in Latin, but it contains a word, "*Ohum*," that is not a Latin word.[7] There is no clear explanation why the

---

[4] King's date of birth was obtained from the Library of Congress Online Catalog, which also supplies Henry as his middle name. The LC Catalog also notes a medical book published by King in 1890. All biographical information about King is derived from his memoir.

[5] King, 100–101 (servants [King does not use the word, "slave" to describe the family domestics, but because they address him as "Mass John" and because slaves are sometimes described as servants I assume that the King family owned some slaves], 15–16 (joins army). King claims his father opposed secession (16).

[6] An extensive search of the *Atlanta Journal Constitution* online archive did not turn up an obituary for King. The search did find an article about the Confederate Soldiers Home that mentioned Dr. King. A search of various genealogical archives available online also failed.

[7] After describing the body lice races the POWs at Camp Chase held to amuse themselves, King remarks (94), "Virgil looking on such a scene would hardly have exclaimed, '*Dens fecit hace Ohum vobis.*'" A seach Virgil's works online indicates that the word "dens" is not used in Virgil's major works. King might be alluding to "The Gnat" or "Culex," a minor work attributed to Virgil, in which the ghost of a gnat returns to remonstrate with a man whose life the gnat has saved at the loss of its own life. It is also possible that there is an author's or printer's error and that "dens" should be "deus," and that the quote is in "pig Latin." If this were the case, the quote might be read as "Virgil looking on such a scene would hardly have exclaimed, 'God makes these oh hums for us.'" Since Virgil in "The Gnat" appears to lament human callousness, it might fit that he would fail to make light of the POWs' lice races. It is also possible that King is alluding to Virgil in Dante's *Divine Comedy* because King mentions this work twice (84, 88). The author wishes to acknowledge the assistance of Dr. John Lawless, Fr. Paul Seaver, O.P. and Fr. Nicholas Ingham, O.P. in trying to resolve this puzzling quotation.

Latin is quoted incorrectly: it could be simply a misquotation or it could be something King picked up during his POW experience. King refers to two Bible verses: on page 48 he refers to Luke 15:22 and 30, and on page 62 he refers to Acts 9:36. King also cites secular material in his book, on page 77 he refers to a Confederate POW memoir in *The Century Magazine* for 1891.[8] On pages 84 and 88 he refers to Dante's *The Divine Comedy*, and on pages 91–92 he refers to Robert Burns' poem, "To a Louse."

Structure of the Narrative

The narrative is chronological, starting with King's reasons for enlisting, then moving on to his first campaigns in which he saw much action on the front lines with the infantry. The largest section of the memoir (chapters two and three) describes his capture, transportation to Camp Chase, and his three hundred days of internment. The narrative seems to end when King returns to his home, but the description of his return is followed without a break in the text by a twelve page criticism of Reconstruction. It is possible that King may have considered Reconstruction a continuation of his internment.

Construction of the Narrative

The text is written from a single constructed perspective. It is written as it was remembered in a chronological fashion. The text was aimed at criticizing the Union and its treatment of Confederate POWs. The Confederate camps had been criticized, but according to King the Union ones were no better. King wrote his memoir to show the hardships he experienced at the Northern internment prison, Camp Chase. The primary purpose of the narrative selections is the author's intention to illustrate Northern attitudes towards the Confederates, which King characterizes as "The mean, vindictive, cowardly spirit of the Yankees...."[9] He does not play up his role in the prison so that he looks like a hero: indeed, he seems to tell his experience of being a POW from the role of an observer. King portrays himself as a victim, he does not blame himself for being captured, nor does he feel inadequate as a soldier in failing to do his duty by being captured. He blames

---

[8] Dr. John A Wyeth, "Cold Cheer at Camp Morton," *The Century Magazine* (April 1891); a reply to Wyeth's memoir and a rejoinder by Wyeth appear in the September issue. King spells Wyeth as Wyath.

[9] King, 103.

his "heartless keepers" for their ill treatment and uncivilized treatment of their prisoners.[10]

Contents of the Narrative

The narrative begins with King's explanation of his reasons for going to war. He tells a little bit about his home and his family, and his father's opposition to secession. He also mentions that one of his brothers died in battle, another died from the disease he picked up in the army, and his third brother was severely wounded while serving in the army[11]. King describes his battle experience in Kentucky, East Tennessee and Mississippi as mostly boring sieges and extended periods of waiting for something to happen.[12] He describes the siege of Vicksburg and his parole after the surrender.[13]

After a brief visit home, King reenlists, is wounded in battle and falls behind Union lines.[14] Only one Union soldier tries to get him medical attention and the Union surgeons ultimately decide that King is not worth trying to save.[15] King explains that he is forced to haul himself to a cabin on a hill where one older woman nurses him until Union soldiers come to take him away to a POW camp. King remembers fighting to keep the pillow the woman gave him as a reminder of her kindness.[16] The soldiers who took him to prison were very abusive even though he was still wounded and recovering. King recalls harsh treatment in his journey to his ultimate destination of Camp Chase, in Ohio.[17]

In the internment camp there was very little food, a sore point to King because, as he remarks on more than one occasion, there was no Sherman or Sheridan in the North slaughtering animals and destroying crops that could have been used to feed POWs. There was very little meat served to the prisoners at Camp Chase; their diet was very poor according to King.[18] Blankets were scarce, and fires were not allowed in the camp, so the prison-

---

[10] Ibid., 73; only one ambulance driver is described as considerate and King notes "…he was quite an exception to the class of ruffians who had been my guards and tormenters and who disgraced the uniform of Federal soldiers" (King, 65–66).

[11] Ibid., 17.

[12] Ibid., 19–30; King's description of the Unionists in East Tennessee is notably hostile, 20–22.

[13] Ibid., 31–46.

[14] Ibid., 47–54.

[15] Ibid., 56–57.

[16] Ibid., 59–61.

[17] Ibid. 62–70.

[18] Ibid., 75–76, 79; Sherman, 3–4, 8; Sheridan, 7–8, 11.

ers were often very cold. They were kept in small huts in which small bunks were stacked. Inside the camp there was very little medical attention or supplies, there were however, hospitals outside of the camp that prisoners were sent to if they were very ill.[19]

King describes escape attempts by the prisoners, when the food wagons would enter the camp the main gates would open, and some prisoners would give the Rebel yell and run out the gates. There was no discussion of elaborate tunnels or escape plans that some others attempted. Prisoners would simply make a run for it, but they were very rarely successful, because the Union soldiers would pursue the prisoners on horseback, often killing them. If the prisoners who attempted to escape were not killed in the pursuit they would be dealt with severely. Punishments were harsh in the camp, and sometimes unwarranted.[20]

The prisoners in Camp Chase were forced to make their own entertainment while they were there. They would make their own chess and checker sets and play games including lice races. Since they were not forced into labor, the POWs had lots of free time. One of the most amusing ways the prisoners would deal with their boredom was to hold a prisoner's ball when the weather was warm enough. They would designate who were the men and who were the "women" by dressing up some of them with blankets and such to distinguish who the "women" were. For the most part the guards found this highly amusing and allowed these balls to happen. The prisoners would play music and hold this dance in the streets of their camp.[21]

King does not go through any conversion while in Camp Chase; he remains a bitter prisoner but he does not attempt to escape because he saw what happened to others who tried to escape. After three hundred days of internment, King returned home. When King arrived his father wasn't home, but he is welcomed by the servants. Later when his father returns, he tells King that he wouldn't have recognized him if he hadn't been told that his son had returned home.[22] Whether this coming home episode is an inversion of the Parable of Prodigal Son or not, it serves to emphasize the effects of the hardship King endured as a Union POW, and to dramatize the hard homecoming that awaited a Confederate veteran.[23]

---

[19] King, 74–75.
[20] Ibid., 85–86, 80–84.
[21] Ibid., 91–95
[22] Ibid., 100–102.
[23] Ibid., 48 alludes to the Parable of the Prodigal Son (Luke15:22–30) in describing his homecoming after he was paroled following the Battle of Vicksburg.

Conclusion

Dr. King's objective for writing this book about his experiences as a POW was to criticize the Union for the way they ran their POW camps. He was very angry at how the Confederate internment camps were portrayed. King thought the public had many misconceptions about conditions during the Civil War. The Union waged a propaganda campaign that made the Confederates look like uncivilized and brutal men, while at the same time General Sherman and General Sheridan tore through the South burning and pillaging. These facts disturbed Dr. King greatly and he was trying in his own way to set the record straight as he saw it.

Although King complains constantly of the ill treatment and conditions of Camp Chase, it seems as though they might be slightly exaggerated in his memory. It does not stand to reason that ill treated and seriously malnourished prisoners would have the strength to hold balls such as King describes.[24] Due to the length between the years that Dr. King spent as a POW and the time when he wrote the book I believe that his memory had embellished the severity of some of the hardships the prisoners faced. King has a considerable grievance with the Union, and he still believes that the Confederate's cause was just. It does not appear that he made up events, or lied about his experiences because he can describe them in great detail, and because he describes some events, such as the balls, that seem to refute what he claims.

---

[24] In much more severe prison camps such as the ones run by the Japanese or the Koreans the prisoners were very malnourished and abused, and all they concentrated on was survival. None of them would even have dreamed of trying anything like holding a ball, they simply did not have the energy for that.

Amos E. Stearns:
Prisoner at Andersonville

A Civil War Memoir

JESSICA PILKINGTON

The Text

THE AUTOBIOGRAPHY, *Narrative of Amos E. Stearns, A Prisoner at Andersonville* explains what Stearns and fellow soldiers experienced while at the mercy of their Confederate captors. The autobiography published by Franklin P. Rice (publisher) in 1887 was intended originally to be a part of *Story of Company A, Twenty-Fifth Regiment, Massachusetts Volunteers* compiled by Samuel Putnam.[1] Putnam, who was Stearns's sergeant, noted in the introduction to Stearns's *Narrative* that *Prisoner at Andersonville* "should have found a place in the *Story of Company A, Twenty-Fifth Regiment, Massachusetts Volunteers*, and was so intended, but circumstances prevented."[2] The diary on which Stearns's *Narrative* seems to have been based was published in 1981.[3]

Three articles about Stearns's *Narrative* have been published since the 1970s.[4] A search of the Historical New York Times and the Making of America Collections of 19th Century journals using "Amos Stearns" failed to turn up any reviews of *Prisoner at Andersonville* or any references to the author. While *Prisoner at Andersonville* was intended to be a part of a work

---

[1] Worcester, Mass: Putnam, Davis and Co., 1886.

[2] Stearns, 7: It has not been possible to determine the nature of the circumstances to which Putnam refers. *Story of Company A* . . . quotes a letter by Captain Emerson Stone who was captured at the same battle as Stearns, 282–83.

[3] Amos E. Stearns, *The Civil War Diary of Amos E. Stearns, a Prisoner at Andersonville*, ed. Leon Basile (London: Associated University Press, 1981).

[4] Both the MLA Index and America History & Life (AH&L) were searched February 21, 2006.

written by all of his fellow soldiers, it provides a clear and dispassionate description of an individual's experience in what is considered one of the worst Civil War prisons.

The Author

Amos E. Stearns (1833–1912) was born in Taunton, Massachusetts on January 9, 1833.[5] Stearns received a basic education, and worked as a machinist. But personal tragedy caused a change of direction in Stearns' life. Stearns' daughter, Mary, died in 1860, his wife (also Mary) in July of 1861, and his other daughter Nellie only one month later. During this time, Stearns lost his job. It was this string of tragedies which made Stearns volunteer as a private for the 25th Massachusetts infantry. Stearns was captured by Confederate forces on May 16, 1864 at the Battle of Drewry's Bluff.[6] After the war, Stearns once again found work as a machinist. He married Lydia Maria Fisher in 1866, and they adopted a son, Walter, in 1873. Stearns published *Prisoner at Andersonville* in 1877. He remained active in veterans' organizations until his death on May 28, 1912.

Framing of the Narrative

A microfiche copy of Stearns's *Narrative* was used for this examination. In the text there are no endorsements, quotations, drawings, maps, or visual aids of any kind in *Prisoner at Andersonville*. The only visual is a photograph of Stearns himself on page four. The microfiche copy of the photograph is too blurred to accurately see, but it appears to be the same photograph that Basile included in his edition of Stearns's diary which is dated to 1875.[7] On the basis of an examination the copy of the original text at the American Antiquarian Society it seems unlikely that Stearns' memoir had a dust cover.

Structure of the Narrative

Amos E. Stearns makes no mention in *Prisoner at Andersonville* of his life prior to his imprisonment. Also, Stearns book is not broken up into chapters, being a brief 57 pages long. It is entirely chronological, beginning at his capture on May 16, 1864, and ending with his return to Worcester, Massachusetts on March 25, 1865 (he was officially paroled on February

---

[5] Biographical information taken from: Stearns, ed. Basile.
[6] About seven miles south of Richmond, Virginia.
[7] Stearns, ed. Basile, unnumbered page ii.

27, 1865). Stearns narrative contains no flashbacks or flash forwards. There is also no discernable turning point in this narrative.

Construction of the Narrative

Prisoner at Andersonville is short, succinct, and to the point. Stearns does not use any quotations from other authors or the Bible. In fact, Stearns's autobiography is different from many others in that he only briefly mentions any personal difficulties from his internment. He mentions terrible rations, shelter, and the misbehavior of guards, but he does not mention how they affected him. As previously noted, Stearns never mentions how his internment made him feel because he acts as more of an outside, omnipotent narrator who explains what happened. The reader does not get the impression that the internment affected him.[8]

There is one metaphor that Stearns uses. Sometimes when a fellow POW died, he referred to death as "answering the great roll call above."[9] But Stearns only uses this expression in the second half of the book. Stearns describes even S.P. Champney, his friend throughout his Andersonville experience, as just "dying" instead of "answering the great roll call above." It seems as those who survived Andersonville but died in Charleston or Florence "answered the great roll call from above" rather than dying.

Contents of the Narrative

As mentioned previously, Stearns makes no note of his life before his capture in his narrative. A quote from Stearns in Putnam's introduction does give a hint as to why he chose the Twenty-Fifth Massachusetts. Stearns noted that he felt that the leaders of this particular regiment were experienced.[10] His wife and children had also just died and he was out of work. Ironically, it seems that the army and even his POW experience was for Stearns an escape from even more wrenching personal tragedies. Because of his years in the army he was able to pay off his $100 debt, and finally purchase gravestones for his family. For Stearns, the army almost provided a happier existence!

Because Stearns memoir is so emotionally detached, he is able to paint not only a very altruistic picture of himself, but also of nearly everyone around him. Stearns rarely uses any terms that denote feelings (the only

---

[8] Distancing can be a strategy for coping with trauma.
[9] Stearns, 47.
[10] Ibid., 6–7.

"feeling" he really talks about is starvation). Discussing his capture, Stearns explains that he was assisting a wounded comrade when they accidentally walked upon a company of Confederate soldiers. He places no blame on himself, his wounded comrade, or the Confederate forces that captured him.[11]

Stearns was first taken to Libby Prison in Richmond, Virginia after he was captured. Here the men were stripped off all their possessions, especially their valuables and Northern money (Confederate money by this point was virtually worthless). Stearns comments on how a member of his company was shot by a guard through his right arm for sitting on a window sill to cool off.[12] At Libby Prison rations were decreased daily.

On May 23rd (a week after his capture), Stearns and the fellow prisoners were placed on the train that took them to Andersonville Prison in Georgia. Stearns recalls that ". . . during all our long ride from Richmond to Andersonville we were not allowed to get off the train to get a drink of water. . . . There were times while on the way that I was so thirsty that my tongue became very much swollen."[13] Yet this train ride was nothing compared to what he and his fellow prisoners were to encounter while at Andersonville Prison itself.

According to Stearns there was a shortage of shelter (called "shebangs") at Andersonville. He was lucky enough to run into a former member of his regiment, S.P. Champney, who actually had a shebang and was willing to share it with Stearns.[14] Most of Stearns's description of Andersonville focuses on the meager rations. Yet men still tried to make the best of it by making meals and trying to sell them off to other prisoners.[15] To give himself some form of purpose and entertainment, Stearns himself got in the wood business after his friend Champney died at Andersonville.[16]

Stearns paints a positive portrait of Captain Wirz, the Swiss born man who ran Andersonville. When a group of six Union POWs, called "raiders," had killed two men in order to steal their possessions, Captain Wirz conducted a fair trial where the men were found guilty, and then hanged.[17] Stearns in fact never speaks ill of Captain Wirz the man. After the war,

---

[11] Ibid., 9–10.
[12] Ibid., 14.
[13] Ibid., 23.
[14] Ibid., 26.
[15] Ibid., 30.
[16] Ibid., 37–38.
[17] Ibid., 33–35.

Wirz was hanged for what were essentially war crimes against Northern soldiers.

After being at Andersonville for five months, the prisoners at Andersonville were tricked by their Confederate captors and were forced on a train to another POW camp in Charleston, South Carolina (they were told they were going to be paroled and get on a Northern ship at Savannah). The presence of Sherman's army in Georgia made the Confederates fear that Andersonville would be liberated. In the three short weeks that the prisoners were held in Charleston, one thousand prisoners "had gone to answer the great roll-call above."[18]

After Charleston the prisoners were taken to Florence, South Carolina. Stearns actually had more harsh things to say about Florence than Andersonville. He recalls that he witnessed a father see his son die, and the Confederate prison guards, deny a burial for the son. Also Stearns notes, "[T]here was nearly as much suffering here [Florence] from the cold as at Andersonville from the heat."[19] It wasn't until February 27th that the prisoners were sent to Camp Parole in Annapolis, Maryland. Of his release Stearns wrote, ". . . I felt so happy that I ran and jumped the best I could, and tried to shout, but no sound would come. I was so overjoyed. That is what I call joy unspeakable."[20]

Stearns made a point to mention those who were particularly nice to him throughout his experience. He specifically mentions the kindness of Calvin Farnsworth, the conductor of the train that took the emaciated Stearns home, because Farnsworth held Stearns's train until he had time to finish his lunch.[21] S.P. Champney also gets mentioned by Stearns because he provided Stearns with shelter and friendship while at Andersonville. He talks of the joys of the overabundance of food at Camp Parole—he got so much food that he didn't know what to do with it. He even happily referenced how the government paid him for all the time he was captured, even though his enlistment had ended while he was imprisoned.[22]

Although Stearns discusses no ills of Captain Wirz towards his prisoners, he often speaks of how the prisoners acted deplorably toward each other. An example of this is the raiders. Sometimes if a prisoner had extra room in his shebang, he would not share it with others who were suffering unless they could bring some good to him (Stearns commented that most

---

[18] Ibid., 44.
[19] Ibid., 47.
[20] Ibid., 53.
[21] Ibid., 57.
[22] Ibid., 57.

would not allow someone into their shebang unless they had a blanket).[23] Stearns himself set up a wood selling business to pass time, but even the man that Stearns purchased wood from eventually refused to help him.[24] Meanwhile, Stearns makes himself seem almost angelic by occasionally getting water or tobacco for dying prisoners. Stearns himself only met a few genuinely nice people in this experience—S.P. Champney and the conductor of the train on his way home.

Amos E. Stearns was a prisoner for nine months and eleven days. During this time he was so deprived of nutrition that he was a mere ninety pounds upon his return to Worcester, Massachusetts. He ends his narrative by saying that the government paid him for every day he was in prison, even after the day his enlistment expired. He makes no mention of his life after his imprisonment.

Conclusion

According to Leon Basile, Stearns does not mention his own private thoughts or personal feelings from his incarceration, because Stearns possibly considered them "too trivial or too personal to share with the public."[25] As a result, Stearns's POW autobiography is different than other such autobiographies. Many POWs who live to tell the tale write how the experience affected them, generally in a negative way. Because Stearns's work discusses no feeling, his experiences at Andersonville did not seem as bad. Another reason why Stearns's POW experience did not appear that horrible is because of all the personal tragedy he experienced before entering the war. For Stearns, the army provided relief from unemployment, as well as personal tragedy. In the army he would not be reminded of the deaths of his wife and two children. While a POW, he still did not suffer as much as he did prior to the war. All in all, Stearns painted a more neutral picture of Andersonville than other Civil War POWs.

---

[23] Ibid., 25–26.
[24] Ibid., 37.
[25] Stearns, ed. Basile, 7.

Richmond Hobson:
The Sinking of the "Merrimac"

A Spanish-American War POW Memoir

Jason Coulombe

The Text

RICHMOND HOBSON's prisoner of war account was first published in *The Century Magazine* between December 1898 and March 1899. It came in four monthly installments in the magazine, which concentrated on the four separate themes of his journey during the Spanish-American War. The first installment was entitled "The Scheme and the Preparation;" the second installment was entitled "The Run In;" the third installment was entitled "Imprisonment in Morro Castle," and the last part was entitled "Prison Life in Santiago and Observations of the Siege."[1] Besides being published in *The Century Magazine*, this autobiographical piece was also published in book form by The Century Company in New York, in 1899, and has since been reprinted by the Naval Institute Press of Annapolis, Maryland.[2] The book and its chapter structures are based on the format of the magazine.

The story of Richmond Hobson, his crew and the *Merrimac*, dominated the presses between June 5 and July 23, 1898. Between those dates Hobson's story was headlined some seventeen times in the *New York Times*, and titles such as "Hobson, The Hero of Santiago" and "Lieut. Hobson's

---

[1] Richmond Hobson, "The Sinking of the 'Merrimac,'" *The Century Magazine*, a popular quarterly: Part I, vol. 57, issue 2, December 1898, 265–84; Part II, vol. 57, issue 3, January 1899, 427–50; Part III, vol. 57, issue 4, February 1899, 580–604; Part IV, vol. 57, issue 4, March 1899, 752–79. *The Sinking of the Merrimac* (New York: The Century Company, 1899), republished (Naval Institute Press, 1987), hereafter referred to as Hobson.

[2] 1987, with an introduction and notes by Richard Turk.

Deed" were used to promote a sense of national victory and gallantry.[3] However, even with the wide promotion of this story in its day, few examinations of the text exist today. The MLA Index provided no search results, while America History and Life had only two hits, both of which pertained to the mission of the *Merrimac* itself, and not to the narrative text. In a separate search however, W.R. Herrick, Jr. notes that Hobson's writing is "done so with a freshness and vigor characteristic of talented writers."[4] Upon the general examination of both the magazine entries, as well as the book version, this narrative seems to be addressed to the American audience that had been following Hobson's adventures during and after his captivity.

The Author

Richmond Hobson was born on August 17, 1870 in Greensboro, Hale County, Alabama. His father James Marcellus Hobson was a Confederate veteran who was wounded three times at Malvern Hill (Virginia), Chancellorsville (Virginia) and Spotsylvania (Virginia), and was captured and spent the remainder of the war as a prisoner after the engagement at Spotsylvania. His mother, Sarah Croom Pearson, could trace her ancestry back to the *Mayflower*. Both sides of the family were involved heavily in politics, an involvement that would benefit Hobson later in life.[5]

After attending several private schools and Southern University as a young man, Hobson went to the United States Naval Academy from where he graduated in 1889. During a period of a naval revolution of design and thought, Hobson then traveled to Paris, France where he attended the French National School of Naval Design. Upon his return to the United States, Hobson served in the Navy Department in Washington with the Bureau of Construction and Repair. After several requests to travel the world and study naval innovation were denied, Hobson was put in charge of a new postgraduate class in Annapolis, which dealt with naval construction.

With the outbreak of the Spanish-American War on April 21, 1898, Hobson was assigned to William T. Sampson's flagship the *USS New York*. After several attempts to track down Admiral Pascual Cervera's Spanish

---

[3] "Hobson, The Hero of Santiago," *New York Times*, 6 June 1898, p. 1: "Lieut. Hobson's Deed," *New York Times*, 12 June 1898, p. 1.

[4] W. R. Herrick Jr., "The Correspondent's Wars," *Military Affairs*, vol. 32, No. 1, p. 35–36.

[5] Biographical information on Richmond Hobson can be found in the introduction of the Hobson narrative (1987) by Richard Turk, vii–xxv. Turk wrote the entry for Hobson in the *American National Biography*, eds. John A. Garraty and Mark C. Carnes, 24 vols. (New York: Oxford University Press, 1999), 10:899–900.

Richmond Hobson: The Sinking of the "Merrimac"

squadron between April 29–June 1, 1898, the American fleet finally caught up with the Spaniards near Santiago, Cuba. Here Hobson was ordered to help plan a mission which would block the Spaniards and their seven ships in the harbor. The plan was to sink the *Merrimac* in the entry way to the harbor to block the Spanish ships from going in or out. Not only did Hobson plan the mission, but he also volunteered himself to command the ship during this mission. Initially the mission was seen as a failure and Hobson and the crew were taken prisoners by the Spanish. Hobson kept an account of his imprisonment between the days of June 3, 1898–July, 5, 1898. During Hobson's thirty-two days as a POW, he was treated exceptionally well by the Spanish. Hobson's treatment as a POW conflicted with the general stereotype of Spanish brutality and mercilessness characteristic of several American publications before and during the conflict. During Hobson's month of imprisonment he was the headline story in many of the United States newspapers, and upon his arrival back to the United States, Hobson was seen and treated as a national hero. According to Richard Turk, Hobson "had become a national hero. His picture appeared in virtually every paper and magazine; reporters vied with each other to find new adjectives to describe his act of 'splendid daring and magnificent courage' he and his men had performed."[6]

Once back in the United States, Hobson experienced national attention and a new life of politics. In 1907, he entered Congress where he would continue for four terms. Fortunately for his political career, he had many family ties to rely on, and with his marriage to Grizelda Houston Hull, he now had ties to General Leonidas Polk and George Houston. While a member of Congress, he worked to strengthen the United States Navy and to expand the Monroe Doctrine into Asia. Before his death on March 16, 1937, Hobson would receive the Congressional Medal of Honor; organize the American Alcohol Education Association, the International Narcotic Education Association, the World Conference on Narcotic Education, and the Constitutional Democracy Association.

Framing of the Narrative

The book form I used for this research project provides no dust jacket.[7] The book has a plain blue cloth cover, with the United States Naval Institute

---

[6] Hobson, xxvii.
[7] After contacting the Naval Institute Press, I was informed by Susan Brook that no dust jacket existed for the 1987 copy of the narrative. This information was given via telephone on 7 April 2006.

insignia on the cover. There is no dedication in the magazine form of the narrative; however, there is a dedication in the 1987 book. It reads, "To Rear-Admiral William T. Sampson U.S.N." Sampson was the Admiral of the *USS New York*, to which Hobson had been assigned before his captivity during the war.

The text itself only provides a detailed account of Hobson's life from May 29, 1898 to Hobson's day of release, July 5, 1898. The narrative is detailed and provides the reader with a good primary account. There are no major literary differences between the original piece in *The Century Magazine* and the book. Both the book and the magazine provide insightful pictures, graphs and blueprints, which greatly add to the quality of this work. The narrative in *The Century Magazine* contained a total of three maps, seven diagrams, one letter and fifty-one pictures, which help support the text. The narrative in book form contains three less pictures, but does include one additional map. Although both the magazine and book narratives contain insightful pictures and details which help the reader, the magazine is broken down into smaller subsections which are easier and clearer to follow than the book, in which chapters tend to run on with no pauses or breaks.

Structure of the Narrative

The text of Hobson's autobiography begins with his stay on Admiral Sampson's flagship, the *USS New York* on May 29, 1898. During this time, the United States Navy is in pursuit of Admiral Cervera's Spanish squadron, which leads the reader into the story. The memoir in book form and in the magazine is broken into four sections: The first section, titled "The Scheme and the Preparation," deals primarily with the preparations for the *Merrimac*'s mission. In this section there are detailed maps, diagrams, blueprints and analysis of the mission that would take place and how it would be conducted. The second part, titled "The Run In," deals with the overall attempt and completion of the mission. This section provides detail on the completion of the mission, the sinking of the *Merrimac*, the night Hobson and his men spent in the harbor's waters, and their eventual rescue. It also provides detailed pictures of the event and the personal accounts of the men on the ship. The third section, titled "Imprisonment in Morro Castle," deals with his capture by the Spanish and the relationship he forms with them. Again, detailed art provides an excellent complement to the writing. Finally, the forth section, titled "Prison Life in Santiago and Observations of the Siege," deals with the United States invasion of Santiago, Cuba, the fighting that took place between the Spanish and Americans, Hobson's emotional distress from losing some of the Spanish friends he made, and then his ultimate release.

The book flows in chronological order with no breaks or interruptions. The turning point of the book is his rescue/capture by Admiral Cervera. Upon the sinking of the *Merrimac*, Hobson and his men were forced to stay in the waters of the harbor throughout the night. Once he is rescued and then imprisoned, there is a general change with the description of the Spanish from enemy to friend. From the beginning of Hobson's narrative, Hobson is planning to attack the Spanish and to help America win this engagement. With his capture he continues to desire an American victory, but Hobson's attitude changes to that of acceptance, compassion and friendship towards the Spanish.

In contrast to the negative stereotypes of the yellow journalists and anti-Spanish propagandists, the Spanish were kind and treated Hobson and his men with the utmost respect. Although Hobson commonly thinks of escaping, he has nothing but kind words and praise for the Spanish and their exceptional treatment of his men throughout his month long captivity.

Construction of the Narrative

The style of Hobson's *The Sinking of the Merrimac* is simple and plain, but is written in an educated manner. The narrative is written so that average Americans could read the story and understand it. Hobson refrains from military or naval jargon, and commonly illustrates his ideas for clarity. Even the descriptive content of the first two sections in the reading, which dealt with the planning and completion of the mission, Hobson uses graphs, diagrams, maps and blueprints to ensure that all readers understand what Hobson's duty was and what obstacles he faced.

There are no references to any previous writings, whether to biblical texts or previous POW accounts. Hobson more or less takes an approach which was suited to illustrate his captors as kind and honest people. Perhaps his southern heritage has something to do with the adjectives used in his description of Spanish, but he commonly uses words such as honorable (used two times in the text), courtesy/courteous (used ten times in the text) and gallant (used four times in the text) to describe the Spaniards.[8] Even though he has the great respect for the Spanish, including Admiral Cervera,

---

[8] "honorable," *The Century Magazine*, vol. 57 issue 4 580 and 602: "courtesy" and "courteous," *The Century Magazine*, vol. 57, issue 4, 580, 583 (twice), 584, 585, 596 (twice), and 601, and vol. 57, issue 5, 755 and 761: "gallant," *The Century Magazine*, vol. 57, issue 4, 583 and 584, and vol. 57, issue 5, 759 and 775.

and Captains Bustamente and Acosta, Hobson does have some feelings of regret and pity. He often refers to the fact that he wishes he could escape and provide the Americans with the information he has come across to ensure a quick and easy victory for the Americans.

The Content of the Narrative

Richmond Hobson's narrative reflects little on the events before his mission into Santiago harbor. As part of Sampson's fleet, Hobson thought he would be responsible for a ship of indestructible magnitude. Only later would he find just the opposite, that he would have to construct a ship that would sink as quickly as possible to ensure that the Spanish fleet would be trapped in the harbor with no way of escaping and with no way of preparing a surprise attack. It was believed by the United States Navy that if it could isolate the ships, then it would be able to proceed with a land attack. Much of Hobson's focus is on this task, and he becomes even more involved when he volunteers to be aboard the ship when the mission was to take place.

Hobson never referred to his previous life or his family. Even upon his capture, his only concern is his naval family and he wishes he could make sure they knew he was still alive. Later in the narrative, although his every need is attended to (by the way, he mentions the conditions of he and his men some twenty-three times), he still wants to find a way to tell the navy everything he knows about the Spanish, including manpower, artillery, etc., to ensure that the United States can win the island and push the Spanish out. Throughout the entire autobiography, Hobson mentions the word escape some twenty-six times; this includes both the escape from the *Merrimac* after it sunk and his escape from internment. Although escape comes up in his narrative, depression and regret are never mentioned. Perhaps this has to do with the fact that if his mission had been successful bottling the Spanish in the harbor, the navy might not have been able to enter into the harbor to battle the Spanish vessels and a land invasion would have been delayed.

The narrative ends with Hobson's release. Never in the narrative does the reader get a sense of self-promotion, arrogance, or of the narrative being used as an instrument for a political career. It seems that the autobiography was strictly written for the American people and to show that the Spanish were a chivalrous and kind people. In fact, Hobson never says a bad word about the Spanish. After being captured by the Spanish Hobson writes, "my men all had dry clothing . . . their wounds had been dressed, and a good breakfast had been served to them."⁹ Later, upon his release by the Spanish, he writes, "Major Yrles asked in a formal way if I was well and was content with the treatment received. I replied in the affirmative, and he asked if I would ask the same question of my men. They all answered in the same way."¹⁰

With the treatment Hobson received, it was difficult for him to say anything bad about the Spanish. In fact, Hobson was able to form close relationships with some of the Spanish officials. Later in the battle for Santiago, Hobson learned that some of his Spanish friends had died. After Hobson learns of Captain Acosta's death, the Captain of the *Mercedes* and a close friend, he writes, "a great rush of pain and grief swept over me."¹¹ Hobson also noted that his treatment and food was far better then that of even the Spanish soldiers. Because he was allowed to eat in the same area as the Spanish soldiers, Hobson was in a position to make an accurate comparison between the American and Spanish soldiers. He often commented that they looked weak and worn down, and believed the bigger and stronger Americans would win the day.

Conclusion

Richmond Hobson's narrative seems to be different then an atypical POW narrative. Often, many narratives speak about the atrocities, the pain, the suffering, the death, and the malnutrition that surrounded their everyday lives. From concentration camp survival stories, to the men that survived Bataan, POW narratives have predominately been negative in nature. This seems to be the dominant theme with most POW literature except for this one. This piece of literature deals with the positives. Never is death spoken about after Hobson's capture. Initially he and his men felt they would not survive the *Merrimac*'s run, but once in captivity the reader never gets the sense that one could die. Even when some of his men become sick, all the precautions are taken to ensure their survival by the Spanish. As mentioned previously, even though escape is a common word in this narrative, descriptive words such as "honorable," "gallant," and "cheerful" are used by Hobson to describe the Spanish and his men. Never does the reader come across negative words such as "despicable," "horrible," or "ruthless." Perhaps this narrative is expressed in such positive terms because Hobson's captivity

---

⁹ Hobson, from *The Century Magazine*, vol. 57, issue 4, p. 583. Can also be found in book, p. 91.
¹⁰ Ibid., vol. 57, issue 5, 776. Can also be found in book, 180.
¹¹ Ibid., vol. 57, issue 5, 758–59. Can also be found in book, 140.

lasted only thirty-two days. Some POW accounts last for hundreds, if not thousands of days. These accounts tend to be more negative in nature.

For a good portion of the narrative, it deals primarily with his captivity and the relations that followed. With that in mind, this piece was used as an educational and inspirational piece for the American people and a way to help heal Spanish-American relations. His dedication to his job in the navy proves that this was not a propaganda piece or some political motivated writing. Later in life Hobson would become involved in politics, but it seems that family ties proved more beneficial then his storied past. As Congressmen, Hobson was concerned about the naval strength of the United States and did use his expertise and past experiences to help build a bigger and stronger navy, which would benefit the United States in future military conflicts. After reading the narrative of Hobson however, it seems that his main goals dealt with drug and alcohol abuse, and it is here his life should be celebrated.

James Norman Hall:
Flying with Chaucer

A World War I Memoir

LINDSAY WEBER

The Text

JAMES NORMAN Hall writes of his experiences as a World War I prisoner of war in his memoir *Flying with Chaucer*. The book being analyzed in this paper is a first edition copy which was published by Houghton Mifflin Company in 1930.[1] Houghton Mifflin Company, which has its origins in 1832, is today one of the United States leading educational publishers, specializing in "textbooks, instructional technology, assessments, and other educational materials." In addition, the company also produces publications that are reference works, fiction, and non-fiction.

While Hall was a renowned fiction writer, his POW autobiographical account did not appear to receive much attention. Only one book review was found on *Flying with Chaucer* and can be located either on Booklist from 1930 or Wilson Library Bulletin in 1930.[2] In addition, after searching the title, there were no hits in the MLA Index nor America History and Life database.[3] However, his other works, such as his co-authored novel *Mutiny on the Bounty*, the first volume in the *Bounty Trilogy*, received much acclaim when it was published in 1932. Hall was a writer, and therefore it could be assumed that part of his intended audience were the usual readers of his fiction novels. His lack of reviews and dedication to the other three

---

[1] The book was published by the Riverside Press Cambridge in Boston and New York, a subsidiary company of Houghton Mifflin.

[2] The search for book reviews on *Flying with Chaucer* also included the Historical New York Times and Wall Street Journal (searched: March 19, 2006).

[3] The MLA and America History and Life indexes were searched on March 19, 2006.

United States Army Air Corps Pilots with whom he spent time with in POW camp may suggest the account could have been written for them as a memoir as well.

The Author

James Norman Hall was born on April 22, 1887 in Colfax, Iowa. He graduated from Grinnell College in Iowa in 1910 and afterwards moved to Boston to pursue writing. Here he attended Harvard Graduate School so that if he failed as a writer he could teach, and he paid for his classes by doing social work at the Society for the Prevention of Cruelty to Children. Hall who on a vacation to England in the summer of 1914 with the intent to meet his favorite author, Joseph Conrad, when the first World War began.[4] Hall, known for his taste for adventure, enlisted in the British Army. He became a private in the first battalion of the Royal Fusiliers. He was later promoted to lance corporeal and placed in charge of a machine gun section which was sent to France in May 1915. While partaking in one engagement at Loos, everyone in his gun crew was killed, except for Hall. In December 1915, Hall was discharged due to the illness of his father. During this time he wrote of his experiences in *Kitchener's Mob: The Adventures of an American in Kitchener's Army*. He returned to England again in 1916 to re-enlist, this time with the Lafayette-Escadrille, a French-American flying corps use to attract American recruits since the United States had still not officially entered the war. Upon the U.S. entering the war, he became the pilot in the 95th Pursuit Squadron of the United States Army Air Corps, until he was shot down, taken to a German hospital, and then spent the remaining time of the war in a German POW camp. His POW account *Flying with Chaucer* begins at this point.

Hall returned to the United States after his "escape" from the POW camp following the signing of the armistice. In 1920, he moved to the South Seas where he spent the majority of his life on the island of Tahiti. He married in 1925 to Sarah (Lala) Winchester, who was part Polynesian and they had two children, Conrad and Nancy Hall. Hall died of a heart attack on July 5, 1951 in his home in Tahiti.[5] His life was full of literary accomplishments which included his most famous work with long-time friend Charles Nordhoff, "The Bounty Trilogy." Hall published sixteen self-

---

[4] Information found on the "James Norman Hall Home: James Norman Hall, the man." http://www.jamesnormanhallhome.pf/indexen.html.

[5] James Norman Hall's bibliographical information came from Wikipedia, *Encyclopedia Britannica*, and his *New York Times* obituary, July 7, 1951.

authored books and eleven novels co-authored with Nordhoff.[6] His autobiography, *My Island Home*, was published following his death in 1952. This autobiography includes two chapters which give another account of his time as a POW.[7]

Framing of the Narrative

Hall's autobiographical account of his POW experience, *Flying with Chaucer*, has a dust-jacket. It's predominately tan, with a small bit of blue in the upper right hand corner. There is a long cloud bubble on the cover with a book with wings at the top of the cloud bubble. Underneath the book is the following quote.

> Brought down with a bullet through his chest after a flight with seven German planes and a two-mile drop behind enemy lines, the author of 'High Adventure' found his enforced stay in Germany lightened by a battered copy of 'The Canterbury Tales,' his constant companion in prison and during his escape and flight to the frontier.

The quote is followed by his name and then the title in big letters at the bottom. The back of the dust jacket contains advertisements for six other Houghton Mifflin Company books under the heading "Studies in Life and Literature." The left inside of the dust jacket gives a brief 86 word description of Hall, and below that lists five books he wrote. The right side of the dust jacket includes a summary of Hall's book *Mid Pacific*.[8]

Inside the cover page includes *Flying with Chaucer*, James Norman Hall, Boston and New York, Houghton Mifflin Company, The Riverside Press Cambridge, and 1930. In addition to the previously listed information, there is an illustration of a book with wings, similar to the one on the dust

---

[6] As sited on the "James Norman Hall's Home: Books by James Norman Hall." http://www.jamesnormanhallhome.pf/indexen.html Found on March 19, 2006.

[7] James Norman Hall, *My Island Home* (Boston: Little Brown & Company, 1952), chapters 19 and 20.

[8] A historian from Houghton Mifflin was contacted in regards to this book jacket on March 20, 2006. However, they had no information on the book since it is out of print. During an online search, I came across Randall House, a rare bookseller in Santa Barbara, CA. Ron Randall, the owner of Randall House, faxed a copy of the dust jacket to me on March 21, 2006.

jacket on the center of the page. Hall dedicates this book "To Lieutenants' Robert Browning, Charles Codman, and Henry Lewis: Formerly of the United States Air Service. In Memory of Landshut Days and the Escape De Luxe." Readers of *Flying with Chaucer* find out on page eighteen that these men were at the POW camp with Hall and then later that the four "escaped" together the day after the signing of the armistice.

Structure of the Narrative

Flying with Chaucer is divided into five chapters of varying length. The first section is Hall's reflection of why he wrote the following four parts. The remaining three sections are his telling about his POW experience, his "escape" and his time after the war flying over a destroyed Western Front with Chaucer's *Canterbury Tales* at his side. The introduction in the first chapter which describes his reason behind writing the account occurs in the time in which he is writing the book. The second chapter starts at the current time, but by within a page Hall begins to describe his experience as a pilot in the United States Army Air Corps in World War I. From then on the chapters flow chronologically until the second to last page of the book, page 55, Hall comes back to present day and compares his story with Chaucer's *Canterbury Tales*.

Construction and Contents of the Narrative

The account contains several quotations from Chaucer which Hall uses for a variety of purposes. He first quotes Chaucer in his introduction when he concludes his idea of being able to tell a bit of history through writing about oneself, how one came across a book and one's journey with that book within the books pages. On page four he says he fully agrees with Chaucer that "Wher-as a man may have noon audience, nought helpeth it to tellen his sentence." The next time he quotes Chaucer is when he, as the prisoners' chosen librarian, first sorts through the books given to the POWs in an effort to catalog them. He finds a book already open to page 368 of his copy of Chaucer and he quotes a passage. In the fourth chapter, he uses a quote from "The Monk's Tale."

> 'Al-though that Nero were as vicious
> As any feend that lyth full owe adoun,
> Yet he, as telleth us Swetonius,
> This wyde world hadde in subjeccioun,

James Norman Hall: Flying with Chaucer

Both Est and West, South and Septemtrioun."[9]

He finds this passage relative to his experience in Switzerland where he had been reading this portion of *The Canterbury Tales*. Hall quotes from "The Miller's Tale" on page 46 of his account when describing a conversation he had about Chaucer with an Englishman he met upon returning to Paris who also shared his passion for Chaucer.

'This DRONKe MILler SPAK ful SONE aGEYN,
And SEYD-e,"LEV-e BROther OS-e-WOLD,
Who HATH no WYF he IS no COK-e-WOLD,
But I sey NAT therefore that THOU art OON."

The above quote is the only one in *Flying with Chaucer* that is oddly capitalized. His last Chaucer quotation appears on page 53 while he is telling of flying over the destroyed western front a few months after the fighting has ended. The quote is taken from "The Knight's Tale" and is used to show his reflection on the comrades lost on the battlefield.

'And certeinly a man hath most honour
To dyen in his excellence and flour,
Whan he is a siker of his gode name;
Thanne hath he doon his freend ne hum no shame.
And gladder oghte his freend ben of his deeth,
Whan with honour up-yolden is his breeth,
Than whan his name appaled is for age.'

Hall also includes a letter he wrote about his POW experience with the intention of giving it to his grandchildren he hoped to have someday. He wanted them to be able to have the opportunity to know their grandfather's experience as a POW. This letter lasts from page nineteen of his account to approximately half way down on page 21. However, the letter is unfinished and he never gets around to describing his war experience. Instead, all he gets around to writing is his motive for telling his grandchildren about his time during WWI. The motive described in his letter to his grandchildren is very similar to his motive for writing *Flying with Chaucer*. Both motives are his way to leave his mark in the world, so future generations will know his story, because he wishes he had known something of his ancestors' experiences.

Flying with Chaucer is different from most POW accounts. It is probably that this is primarily due to Hall's writing style, keeping in mind that he already had written and published a few other books by 1930. *Flying*

---

[9] Hall, *Flying with Chaucer*, 40.

with Chaucer is styled, rather than a simple narrative. Hall's experience as a POW is presented as a piece which almost mirrors romantic literature. Certain aspects of Hall's experience lead the reader to sense a romantic style in this literary work. For instance, the German prison is located in an old castle called the Schloss Trausnitz in the German province of Bavaria, which adds a vision of chivalry to the audience's mind.[10] The relationship Hall and the other prisoners have with the German guards is civil and at times even friendly. Aside from boredom, the conditions are comfortable, and occasionally better than that of the German guards. However, Hall's relationship to Chaucer's *Canterbury Tales* in this story probably is the biggest factor in its literary romanticism. His constant relating of his experiences to Chaucer's own words and tales makes the reader feel as though Hall is going through his journey as a POW with a close friend at hand. The reader gets a sense of comfort in what could be a more uncomfortable situation. Another way of viewing it is that Hall is comparing his experience to a pilgrimage like the one which is described by Chaucer's characters. So his finding Chaucer's book during an experience he viewed as like a pilgrimage adds a sense of irony to his story.

However, interestingly, Hall in his full life autobiography *My Island Home* only mentions Chaucer twice in the three chapters of the book dedicated to the same incidents discussed in *Flying with Chaucer*. He quotes from the Miller's Tale while describing a conversation he had in Paris with the Englishmen.[11] Hall then quotes from "The Knight's Tale" when he described his thoughts and emotions during his last flight over the front in France.[12] Although there are two quotations in his full-life autobiography, according to *Flying with Chaucer,* the importance of Chaucer in his life during this time appears to be greatly downplayed in *My Island Home*. It makes the reader question whether or not the emphasis of Chaucer in *Flying with Chaucer* was more of a literary exercise than an accurate account.

In the second chapter of *Flying with Chaucer*, Hall leaves his current time and his discussion of his motives for writing the account to dive into how he became a POW. Hall begins his account with describing that he became a POW while flying over enemy territory when his plane was shot down. He spent six weeks in a German hospital recovering from serious injuries from his crash. While Hall never expressed guilt or blame for his capture, he does briefly state that the adaptation to internment proved to be difficult at first and that he spent the early days of captivity in a "kind

---

[10] Hall describes the castle and its history on page 6 of *Flying with Chaucer.*
[11] Hall, *My Island Home*, 221.
[12] Ibid., 226.

of waking dream."¹³ As previously mentioned, the conditions were comfortable for the men at Schloss Trausnitz. They had decent food, especially when packages were sent by loved ones from home and the Red Cross. Boredom, on the other hand, was a big issue, so the men of the prison asked for English books and this was granted. It was by this request that Hall came across his companion, Chaucer. Hall continues to explain the changes at the prison, including the departure of all prisoners, except for Hall and the three lieutenants to which this book is dedicated.

After the signing to the Armistice, the four prisoners begged the inspector of prison camps in Bavaria, Herr Pastor, to release them, although no orders had been given to Pastor to release the prisoners. The inspector's decision was to allow an "escape de luxe."¹⁴ De Luxe means "of luxury" in French, so one could translate this as they had a luxurious escape. The men "escaped" to Switzerland where they ran into a little trouble because of leaving prison camp early, but they were eventually sent to Paris to report back to duty. Hall is not enthusiastic about reporting back for duty after spending time as a POW, and he asked himself how he could "…best bring my own career as a soldier and airman to a fitting and memorable close."¹⁵ However in Paris, Hall requested to take one last flight over the Western Front. The account ends with Hall's reflection on the devastation of the war and the extraordinary losses of great men. Of course, his beloved Chaucer was taken along for the flight and rested in the seat next to him. He put his experiences of war to rest with this final flight and was able to "say goodbye forever to the Air Service."¹⁶

Conclusion

It appears that Hall is trying to put closure to a period in his life. While this account is published twelve years following the close of the war, often veterans are still haunted by memories of war, and this may be an opportunity for him to close this chapter in his life. Clearly, his flight over the Western Front was his attempt to do just that in the close aftermath of the war. However, I think his real objective for writing his account as a POW and his journey with Chaucer was to do just what he claimed his motive to be in the first chapter. Hall wrote this account to tell a small bit of his life to people interested in hearing it. It was, as he claims in his letter to his

---

[13] Hall, *Flying with Chaucer*, 7.
[14] As described by Lieutenant Browning in *Flying with Chaucer*.
[15] Ibid., 48.
[16] Ibid.

grandchildren, a personal motive at bottom.[17] This account was his attempt to live longer through the readers of *Flying with Chaucer*. Hall was interested in continuing family stories, as he longed to know ancestors stories and the stories of those who owned his copy of *Canterbury Tales* prior to him. Incorporating *Canterbury Tales* as a means for describing his own experience is quite revealing because for centuries readers have passed down Chaucer's stories, and Hall hopes to do the same with his own.

[17] Ibid., 20.

William A. Berry:
Prisoner of the Rising Sun

A World War II Memoir

MICHAEL S. ENG

The Text

PRISONER OF the Rising Sun was written by William A. Berry with the help of James Edwin Alexander between the winters of 1990 and 1991. It was first published by the University of Oklahoma Press in Norman, 1993. It does not seem that Berry's story was published before 1993.[1]

Berry was a naval ensign during World War II, stationed in the Philippines and captured by the Japanese during the fall of Manila. He states in the book's preface that the motivation for writing his story came from the fact that he wanted the future generations of his family to know his role in World War II, because he had a great interest of his own grandfather's involvement in the American Civil War, yet there were no real recorded documents of their service.

No reference to an article discussing this memoir was found on the America History and Life or MLA Index search engines.[2] A review for the book was found on the database American Search Premier under South East Asia book reviews, written by Michael Laird.[3] As for other reviews, they were virtually non-existent for this account. Upon reading *Prisoner*

---

[1] James Edwin Alexander is identified on the dust jacket as a professor at Oklahoma City University and an investment advisor.
[2] A search of the *New York Times*, the *Oklahoman* archives, as well as *Book Review Digest* and other online search engines came up empty as well (March 13–20, 2006).
[3] Michael Laird, *Asian Affairs*, vol. 25 (June 1994), 218; Joseph Wharton, "A POW's Greatest Trial Was His Own," *American Bar Association Journal*, (May 1995), is a short book notice that focuses on a particular episode in the memoir.

of the Rising Sun, Berry appears to have no particular readers in mind and probably intended the book to be for a general audience.

The Author

Berry does not write extensively about his early life before enlisting with the United States Navy in the summer of 1941.[4] He was born in 1915, and he mentions that his father was in his mid-forties at the time of his birth. Because his father was an older man, Berry writes that he never really became as close as he would have liked with his father because of his father's age and health problems. However, he writes that he maintained a close relationship with his mother.

In the summer of 1941, Berry was twenty-five years old and felt that he "had 'the world on a string and the string around my finger,' to quote an old song."[5] One year out of law school, he describes himself as an ambitious young man. During that time he became the prosecuting attorney for the county seat of Stillwater, Oklahoma. However, world events inspired him to enlist in the Navy as an intelligence officer.

Seemingly without any training, Berry was stationed in the Philippines as a naval ensign. He describes his naval life as routine and boring. When the invasion came, Berry did not play any major role in the actual combat and was eventually captured by the Japanese in May of 1942. From that time forward he was a POW until near the end of the war in 1945.

After the war, he was honorably discharged from the navy with the rank of lieutenant commander and awarded the bronze star of bravery. He returned to Stillwater and entered the private practice as a lawyer. In 1947 he was appointed U.S. Attorney for the western district of Oklahoma, and ran for the U.S. Congress against John Jarman in 1950, losing in a close race.[6] In 1958, he was appointed to the Supreme Court of Oklahoma and served as Chief Justice from 1971–1972. Berry retired from the court in 1979 and lived in Oklahoma City until his death in 2004.

Framing of the Narrative

There is a dust jacket that comes with the book and it has an illustration on the front. It looks to be a painting of several men standing at attention

---

[4] Biographical information on Berry was drawn from *Prisoner of the Rising Sun* by William A. Berry with James Edwin Alexander (Norman: University of Oklahoma Press, 1993), hereafter cited as Berry.

[5] Berry, 3.

[6] Ibid., 225.

William A. Berry: Prisoner of the Rising Sun

around several Japanese flags, while there is an American flag in the blue sky.[7] There are no reviews on the dust jacket and on the back there are pictures of the two authors, William A. Berry and James Edwin Alexander. Alexander is a professor at Oklahoma City University and an investment advisor, according to the dust jacket. The remainder of jacket gives a synopsis of Berry's account.

Throughout the book there are eighteen pictures, one reproduced document, and six maps.[8] The photographs vary from pictures of the Philippines to pictures of the author, before and after the war; the maps indicate the locations described in the memoir and the document is the statement Berry wrote for the Japanese military tribunal before his trial for escaping.

The photograph in the preface is a picture of the author in his naval uniform when he first enlisted. On page 32 there is a picture of Corregidor Island where fighting took place between the United States and Japan during Berry's enlistment. There is a photograph of the Malinta Tunnel on page 37. There is also a picture of guns installed after World War I as a defensive measure for the Philippine islands on page 47. Unfortunately for the United States, the guns were facing the wrong way at the time of the Japanese invasion.

There is a photograph of Berry's mother on page 143 that he carried with him throughout his ordeal as a POW. Twice in the account this photograph is described almost like a talisman that assists Berry in surviving his time as a prisoner.[9] A photograph of the execution chamber at Bilibid Prison can be found on page 154. A reproduction of the author's written statement for his court-martial by the Japanese for attempting to escape the prison can be found on page 159. There are also sketches of the types of cells that prisoners were put in at the Bilibid prison; there are similar sketches like that on pages 178 and 198. The last few photographs are of the author, one taken three weeks after his rescue in 1945 (p. 219) and a photo of Berry as Chief Justice of the Supreme Court of Oklahoma (p. 224).

The book is dedicated to the author's mother and father, Harriet Virginia Berry and Thomas Nelson Berry. There are no quotes used to start chapters or special quotes used throughout the narrative. There is, however, an Appendix at the end of the book that contains seven excerpts that substantiate Berry's account, and an Epilogue that briefly chronicles the postwar lives of many of the people mentioned in the account.

---

[7] The illustration was prepared by the author's son, Neil Berry, Ibid., xiv.

[8] A list of the pictures and the document is on page ix, and a list of the maps is on page x.

[9] Ibid., 100, 142.

MICHAEL S. ENG

Structure of the Narrative

The structure of the narrative is chronological. Berry relies heavily on dialogue between the people involved and himself. The memoir starts with the author's decision to enlist in the summer of 1941 and ends with his return to the United States at the end of the war. The narrative is not interrupted by flashbacks and does not use stream of consciousness. Basically, one could view the narrative as one long flashback.

Construction of the Narrative

The style of the text can be seen as plain and flowing. The author uses vivid language in describing the pain and suffering that he and other POWs went through and he paints a good picture of what the situation was like. However, Berry does not seem angry at the Japanese and reports his interactions with them in a non-biased way. In fact, one can take notice of the author's sense of humor and irony throughout the account; many episodes seem to be included because of their ironic or humorous nature. In one instance, Berry notes how he is issued a gun that he does not even know how to fire.[10] In another ironical twist, Berry seems to dislike his commander, Tom Lowe, more than his captors and even reports episodes when the Japanese seem to have concern for his well-being.[11] He also notes the irony of being recommended for the Purple Heart because he was strafed at a latrine rather than for what he endured as a POW.[12] Shortly after his capture, one of Berry's friends remarks, "The minute we loose our sense of humor, we'll be dead."[13] Humor is described as a tactic for surviving the unpredictable fortunes of war, and humor together with unpredictability produces irony as a constructive element of Berry's narrative.

It does not seem that Berry used other POW accounts as a model for writing the story. He was motivated by the fact he could not find any information about his grandfathers' experiences in the American Civil War and by two other POW accounts written by men in similar situations in the Philippines. Also, in the book's preface Berry is quite critical of the Code of Conduct for POWs that was drawn up by the War Department.[14] He does not agree that POWs should be encouraged to keep fighting; instead he

---

[10] Ibid., 22.
[11] Ibid., 142–44, 148–49, 172.
[12] Ibid., 212–13.
[13] Ibid., 77.
[14] Ibid., xiii; Lowe is a pseudonym, 228.

argues that the others who were not captured should pick up the torch and continue. He does note that since he was writing his narrative fifty years after the fact that some of the details of the events are sometimes hazy in his memory, but he claims he writes to the fullest extent of his knowledge.

Contents of the Narrative

Before his enlistment, as was mentioned before, Berry worked as a lawyer. He had no real formal military training prior to 1941 and even when he enlisted he was not given real military training. The account is reported matter-of-factly, as a lawyer would, giving the facts as to what happened. Although Berry does not demonize the Japanese, he does attribute many hardships to their failure to plan for large numbers of POWs. He does not introduce many of his own emotions into the writing, yet he does have certain hatred towards the officers, especially his commanding officer Tom Lowe, who betrayed him and his fellow escapees.[15] He describes the wretched conditions, poor food, and the sickness that resulted and the harsh treatment he endured when he was recaptured after his escape.[16] Berry's health and physical condition decline under this regime until he realizes, in what he describes as an almost chance insight, that if he fasts until he is delirious, he will be transferred to the infirmary.[17]

The author takes a passive stance throughout the narrative for the most part; but he does attempt to escape and succeeds briefly. He tries to describe himself as a popular easy-going guy who is well-liked by most people. There are few specific episodes that go against his character construction throughout this account.[18]

Conclusion

Expectations going into the reading this book was this would be an account filled with atrocities and horrors that many have come to associate the POW experience in World War II. However, this was not case, Berry seems to have been quite lucky in his ordeal and while he definitely faced many struggles, he was able to the make best of his situation and to survive.

Overall, Berry's account of being a prisoner of war for the Japanese during World War II offers great insight into prison life during this time

---

[15] Ibid., 135–38, 148–49.

[16] Ibid., 210, 172–88.

[17] Ibid., 191–93.

[18] When Berry does describe an incident that goes against his character construction, for example, his annoyance about buying shoes (Ibid. 135), he explains it away.

and is presented by the author in a seamless and fluid manner. The attention to detail that Berry gives, as well as his recall of entertaining anecdotes makes *Prisoner of the Rising Sun* not only a useful historical reference for POWs during World War II, but also an enjoyable read.

Albert Clark:
33 Months as a POW in Stalag Luft III

A World War II Memoir

KYLE CASEY

The Text

ALBERT P. Clark's account of his time in a German prisoner of war camp for Allied airmen during World War II is entitled *33 Months as a POW in Stalag Luft III*.[1] This memoir was published for the first time by the Fulcrum Publishing Company in 2004. I could not find any review of this work, nor a reference to it in America History and Life or the MLA Index. Though he does not indicate the target audience for his book, Clark does mention that relatively few people have experienced the prisoner of war life he led for several years, and he felt it would be appropriate to publish his memoirs for those who would never have his experience.[2] It seems to be a book written for the general public to read. Clark's story was published in 2004, a full fifty-nine years after his repatriation from German prison camps.

The Author

Albert P. Clark was born in 1913 at Schofield Barracks, Hawaii.[3] He graduated from the U.S. Military Academy at West Point in 1936, from where he went to flight school, joining the U.S. Army Air Forces. Although this information is alluded to at certain points in the narrative, Clark only men-

---

[1] Albert P. Clark, *33 Months as a POW in Stalag Luft III: A World War II Airman Tells His Story* (Golden, CO: Fulcrum, 2004), hereafter cited as Clark.

[2] Clark, xv.

[3] Biographical information on Clark is taken from the memoir.

tions that he was a graduate of West Point. At the time of World War II, Clark was a young Lieutenant-Colonel fighter pilot at the age of twenty-nine. After the war was over, Clark continued to serve in the military, working his way up to the rank of Lieutenant-General, and eventually served as the sixth superintendent of the US Air Force Academy at Colorado Springs for four years until his retirement in 1974. He still resides in Colorado Springs, Colorado. This post-war information is found in the "About the Author" section, as the narrative ends with Clark's return to his home in Texas after his repatriation in 1945.[4]

Framing of the Narrative

The copy of *33 Months as a POW in Stalag Luft III* used for this study is a paper-back edition, and to my knowledge a hardcover one does not exist. On the cover is an illustration of Clark crash landing near the French shore of the English Channel, and was created by Clark Lincoln. The back cover review and the foreword were both written by Duane J. Reed, former Archivist at the United States Air Force Academy. Both tell of Clark as a daring senior leader of clandestine and escape operations within Stalag Luft III. Clark in his introduction tells the reader that he wrote his story down because of the insistence of his friends and family, many of whom he acknowledges for their help in editing and publishing his work, including his nephew Clark Lincoln, who drew the illustration on the cover. Clark states that he regrets taking fifty years to write down the experiences that he had, and apologizes in advance for any faded memories. In the preface Clark describes what it meant for a military man to be captured during a war effort, and escape was constantly on the minds of many of his fellow POWs or "kriegies" as the Germans called them. Escape was even considered the duty of British prisoners of war, with whom Clark spent much time during his POW internment.

Within the narrative are 73 pictures, charts, maps, and drawings littered throughout seemingly every page of the book, many of which were produced by Clark himself. The majority of the pictures were taken through clandestine operations, with cameras carefully and secretly packaged and sent to the POWs from the Allied forces on the outside. The vast major of these images are currently held at Air Force Academy Library, a collection that includes these maps, charts and illustrations, as well as pictures taken by the Allies, but also many courtesy of the Germans. Each of the eleven chapters are titled by where Clark is during that point in his narrative, save

[4] Clark, pp. 206–7.

chapter three entitled "Off to the Rodeo" when Clark enters his first battle. Under each chapter title are the dates encompassed for the events of the chapter. Aside from the sections already described, there is a detailed bibliography and index following the narrative.

In the bibliography, Clark lists many books written by others about Stalag Luft III, many of which written by his fellow prisoners. Maybe the most significant of these books is *The Great Escape* by Paul Brickhill, made into a movie nominated for an Oscar in 1963. Although Clark does not mention the Australian Brickhill or his work among those he discusses in his narrative, the book is listed in the bibliography. The movie *The Great Escape*, starring Steve McQueen, and James Garner, is what made Stalag Luft III famous around the world. Clark may have been motivated to share his story because of the popularity and commercial success of the movie and other accounts written about the Great Escape, and Stalag Luft III.[5]

Structure of the Narrative

Clark's memoir follows a strict chronological order, only straying when telling anecdotes about fellow *kriegies*, such as how they were captured or their previous military service. The book begins on June 23, 1942, the day Clark arrives in England, and the narrative ends on the twenty-sixth of May 1945, the day Clark arrives home in San Antonio, Texas. The book proceeds in a chronological fashion, describing the important events, stopping briefly sometimes to describe in detail certain aspects of POW life, such as food, morale, entertainment, family, stories of the kriegies, and most importantly escape business, efforts, and attempts. The narrative ends fittingly, in the arms of his family, as he had dreamed of being with them for so long. Although the climax of the story is the liberation to prison camp Stammlager VIIA, in Moosburg, Germany by American Forces, the resolution of the story occurs within the very last few sentences of the narrative, when Clark finally reunites with his family a couple of months later.

Construction of the Narrative

Clark's narrative is a very simple one, not filled with metaphors or biblical quotations. The theme of the story, though not stated explicitly, can be found in Clark's introduction and preface, where he talks about the friend-

---

[5] Clark does not mention any where in the narrative these reasons as an influence to share his account, however, he does stand in a unique position because of the fact that most published accounts of Stalag Luft III are British, and that Clark was a high-ranking officer and also was imprisoned longer than all but a handful of men during World War II.

ships and bonds he formed, along with the common goal of escape and survival amongst all the different men, from different nations and backgrounds that he was imprisoned with for nearly three years. Clark mentions that as a result of his POW experience he " . . . gained a clearer recognition of the value of teamwork," and that his " . . . former ardor for rapid advancement cooled."[6] Clark's memoir is, therefore, both a story of survival and a story of growth. Through out his work Clark is very careful to cite other works, as there are many accounts written about Stalag Luft III, and the famous Great Escape from the camp that took place in March of 1944. Clark uses other works and stories cleverly adding other's amazing stories to his work, as well as giving credibility to many of his claims.

Clark depicts himself in his memoir as life-long military man, through and through. He loved the Army, and he loved to fly. Clark did not describe his life at all outside of the military, and the only time he strayed from talking about life in the military or as a POW was when talking about his wife.

The Contents of the Narrative

The vast majority of Clark's account is a chronological one in which he describes where he was, what he saw and experienced, and most importantly who he met. Clark is very specific about the events leading up to his capture. He recalls with some bitterness that his English Allies were not very helpful in introducing Clark and his American pilots to their new British Spitfire aircraft, as well as the enemy German aircraft and combat-style. He goes into great detail to describe that because of his rank he was not bunked with his squadron at the airfield in England, and therefore missed out on the conversation amongst his fellow pilots. Clark mentions that his plane had to be repaired as he had popped some rivets in its tail. Over drinks the British Group Captain informed him that when landing on rough fields such as ours, one must avoid holding the tail down hard, as the Spit had a weakness in its tail bulkhead. "I would like to have known this sooner, but there were lots of things we hadn't yet learned about our new aircraft and air fighting."[7] The next day, he received a replacement plane, borrowed from another airfield, "I was not happy about the loss of my aircraft. We all knew that when one gets a borrowed aircraft from a unit not your own, one never gets the best one."[8] The following day Clark would fly this plane into

---

[6] Clark, xvi.
[7] Ibid., 15.
[8] Ibid., 15.

combat for the first time, and the placement of this section at the very end of its chapter seems deliberate, as the next chapter is about his capture.

His mission on July 26, 1942 was to sweep with his squadron over Abbeville, a town on the English Channel, in northwest France. Because he was housed away from the other pilots Clark was not informed of a pre-flight briefing the morning of his first combat. "We would proceed with radio silence, at minimum altitude, using 1,800 RPM to save gas, until we were close to the French coast. I was to stick close to Green throughout the mission. That was all I knew when we went out to start engines. I had no time to express my anger and indignation at the failure by Green and Squadron leader Weston to arrange for me to get to the briefing. They had just forgotten about me."[9] After brief initial contact with enemy aircraft taking-off, Clark describes his excitement and eagerness to find a dogfight, however, he explains that this was his fatal error because the planes sped back to England. "If I'd had the benefit of the briefing, I would have known that our quick exit from the area was a prerequisite for survival."[10] Clark comes off as a very proud man, who is ashamed of his initial capture, particularly since it was his very first engagement with the enemy. Through this entire section of the memoir it is clear that Clark blames the jaded British Royal Air Force, who had been engaged with a full-scale war with the Germans for years, for how poorly he and eager men were prepared for battle. Clark does not fail to mention and even to praise the German Luftwaffe for their superior skills and aircraft.

Clark was interned in Stalag Luft III where the *kriegies* (POWs) were fed well, treated decently, had proper clothing, and could send and receive mail and packages at their leisure.[11] They were able to even play instruments, and put on performances in a 500 seat theater they built.[12] The morale in this prison camp seemed very high because there is no mention of suicide within the camp, and almost no mention of deaths. The vast majority of the soldiers were kept very busy with clandestine operations, and even if they weren't intimately involved, which Clark was, the prisoners were helpful in many ways. The officers were in charge of specific aspects of the great variety escape operations such as: counterfeiting, photography, clothing making, tunnel digging, construction, and creating general distraction and mayhem in the camp.

---

[9] Ibid., 17.
[10] Ibid., 19.
[11] Ibid., 44–46.
[12] Ibid., 107.

It is very interesting how Clark describes life inside the prison camp, for it truly does not seem that bad.[13] Although Clark missed his family a great deal, and he wished to be flying in combat missions again, the way in which Clark talks about his life as a POW and the lives of his comrades, suggests that they seemed to enjoy their lives as military men *inside* the prison camp. Whether they were working on means of escape, getting away with illegal activities, collecting materials and articles about the war, or simply playing with the prison guards, the *kriegies* were truly part of the war effort. They kept their captors very busy, and were able to transmit invaluable information to the Allied forces via a sophisticated system of code and through escape even though they knew that they could be caught and punished.

The bulk of the story is about the men that Clark was imprisoned with, particularly the officers, since they were the ones he was detained with. He talks of their lives in the military, their stories of capture, espionage, and valor, just as when telling of his own life, he omits almost all details of the lives of his fellow *kriegies* except for ones of war. Clark sections off areas of the story where he describes his role in the Stalag. One such instance took place soon after first arriving to the camp when Clark volunteered to clean up the latrines, which were filthy, smelly, and directly responsible for the spread of disease around the camp. Because Clark had spent summers with his surgeon father at a Colorado base, he had " . . . often accompanied Dad when he inspected the camps, and I learned what a clean and fly-proof latrine should look like and how it should be constructed."[14] Clark assembled a crew of volunteers to do just this to the Stalag's latrines and he mentions these volunteers were of a wide multinational variety, with the glaring exception of the British.[15] Clark's improvements were a hit around the camp, and his effort became known as "Clark's Crap in Comfort Campaign." The Germans incorporated these improvements in the latrines of all four of the

---

[13] On page 105 of Clark's memoir there is a photograph of Sergeant Glemnitz, the senior noncommissioned officer in charge of security at the camp. The legend under the photograph reads "This photo was taken through a louver in the attic of one of our blocks without Glemnitz's knowledge. I showed it to him at one of our reunions and he was astounded." It is not unusual for POWs to have reunions, but it does seem unusual that one of the internment guards would be invited to attend. The invitation and the attendance of Glemnitz suggest a level of mutual respect that speaks to how the POWs were treated.

[14] Ibid., 47.

[15] Clark takes the opportunity several times during the story to take a shot at the British, as he seems to blame them for his capture. However, at several points during the narrative Clark commends the British for their undying optimism in escape attempts and also for their camaraderie.

future compounds built at Stalag Luft III, and the commandant mentioned Clark's work in his memoirs."[16]

Another area that Clark describes is his role in escape plans. Roger Bushell, the British jail-break mastermind, gave Clark ". . . the task of providing secure hiding places for our inventory of escape equipment. I became known as 'Big S.' We knew that in the spring when we moved to the new camp the Germans would search each of us thoroughly. The task of getting our money, false travel papers, tools, compasses, maps, and civilian clothing through the search would be a formidable one."[17] Clark describes in detail the many roles, responsibilities, dangers, and tasks associated with the enormous escape efforts in the camp, and this role as 'Big S' was how Clark fit into the system.

At this point in the narrative Clark begins to describe his hobby of creating a scrap book. This became an obsession of his, and also his greatest treasure. "I had started a collection of clippings from the German newspapers and magazines . . . photographs of Hitler and all of the key figures in the German government. This was soon followed by an effort to obtain photos of all the German army, navy, and Luftwaffe generals and other national heroes. . . . Then the collection inexorably broadened to include clippings of all the German weapons, from the smallest to the largest, and all of the aircraft."[18] The scrap book would continue to grow into a second volume, and would include Clark's notes, sketches, and letters among other important items. These scrap books would prove essential in his narrative writing process. Clark mentions Lt. Col. Willy Lanford as the man directly responsible for the survival of the scrap books. When the camps were abandoned in January of 1945, the *kriegies* had to pack all of their essential belonging and carry them or put them on a sled, and bring them along on a week long forced march that stretched over forty miles in the dead of winter. Weighing over twenty pounds together, Clark on many occasions wanted to leave them behind to lighten the load of their sled, but recognizing their value, Lanford refused each time.

The story does have a dramatic turn on January 27, 1945, with the nearing of the Russian soldiers to the East. The guards and prisoners of Stalag Luft III in Sagan, Germany[19] abandoned their camp. Their destination was Moosburg in Bavaria, the most southwestern province of

---

[16] Ibid., 48.

[17] Ibid., 70.

[18] Ibid., 80–81.

[19] Sagan is in the region known as Silesia, north of Czechoslovakia, and on the border of Poland. Today the town is called Zagan, and is part of Poland.

Germany. In order to get to Moosburg the men would need to reach a train in Spremberg, over fifty miles from Sagan. To get to Spremberg the men were forced to march in the dead of winter for seven days, clearly the absolute worst week of Clark's imprisonment. "We were being pushed hard by the goons, as all of the other columns were following us, and the five camps must have stretched out for twenty miles. There was a possibility that the Russians might overtake us. In violation of the Geneva Conventions, which specified that POWs were not to be marched more than twelve and a half miles in twenty-four hours we were marched thirty-five miles in twenty-seven hours."[20] Not only was the marching itself terrible, but also because of the fact that the Russians were so quickly approaching, the Germans were caught by surprise, and didn't have any arrangements for shelter, food, or hot water, only adding to the dreadful misery of the trek. Arriving in Spremberg on February 2nd, the *kriegies* were loaded into filthy train cars previously transporting cattle, and headed for Moosburg.

From February 5th, until May 12th 1945, the former prisoners of Stalag Luft III, now were joined with the prisoners from many other prison camps in Stammlager VIIA, holding around 30,000 Allies POWs. This camp was very different than the Stalag, as it was absolutely filthy.[21] It was invested with disease and many different kinds of bugs and lice. All the men were sick, and the fact that all the men were on half rations certainly didn't help. Conditions in April improved a little as the American forces drew closer and closer daily. The prisoners had more freedom, and the guards didn't pay nearly as much attention to clandestine efforts as they once did, for both sides knew the camp would soon be liberated, so what was the point of escape. Clark even mentions a forged pass he had that allowed him to go to a storage facility in town a mile away. He walked around observing German life, and not a soul care, the war was clearly on its last legs.[22]

Conclusion

While I believe that feelings that Clark expressed as a prisoner in his account, *33 Months as a POW in Stalag Luft III* were very characteristic of a captured man at war, the story of his time at the POW camp is I believe is entirely unique. Every man passionate about battle and his country will feel guilty for being caught by the enemy, every man will dream of reuniting with his wife and children, and every man would love the opportunity

---

[20] Clark, 146.

[21] A picture on page 161 does an excellent job showing the condition of the camp.

[22] Ibid., 169–72.

Albert Clark: 33 Months as a POW in Stalag Luft III

to get back in action to fight for their nation. These are the sentiments expressed by Clark in his account, however, his POW account is strikingly different for two main reasons: first because it is so consumed with the prospect, the duty of escape, and second because he and his fellow prisoners were treated so well. While most POW's will think about escape every now and again, looking for the perfect opportunity should it arise, most cases are not like that of Stalag Luft III, where the mind of almost every prisoner was on the project of escaping. Everyone was involved in one way or another in a well-oiled escape machine.

Escape for these POW's seemed like it might be unnecessary because of how well these men were treated. They led very comfortable lives in the Stalag, they were fed well, had several changes of clothes, and allowed their own entertainment among other things. This doesn't sound like the life of men captured in war. The POW's in Stalag Luft III were treated well enough that they could focus on escape, rather than on survival, like so many others in a POW situations, and this opportunity to work and plan with a diversity of soldiers was for Clark a transforming lesson in teamwork.

Dorothy Danner:
What a Way to Spend a War

A World War II Memoir

BRIGID MCDONOUGH

The Text

DOROTHY STILL Danner's autobiography, *What a Way to Spend the War: Navy Nurse POWs in the Philippines*, was published in 1995 by the Naval Institute Press in Annapolis, Maryland. Danner wrote the autobiography by herself, but she acknowledges the fact that she could not have written her autobiography without her "Navy nurse peers, other ex-POW Army and Navy personnel, and civilian internees who have shared their memories with me."[1] This is probably primarily because of the half century that had passed since she had been a Navy nurse and POW in World War II and when she decided to write her autobiography.

The Naval Institute Press, which published Danner's autobiography, has a long outstanding reputation of excellence in publishing. "For more than 130 years, USNI has been nurturing creative thinkers who responsibly raise their voices on matters relating to national defense."[2] It is the publishing division of the U.S. Naval Institute: The Independent Forum on the Sea Services and National Defense, and they publish 70 titles yearly. "With its long-established tradition of publishing excellence in the fields of naval, military, and maritime history, the Naval Institute Press provides the serious reader with an invaluable resource."[3] The Naval Institute Press has

---

[1] Dorothy Danner, , *What a Way to Spend a War* (Naval Institute Press, 1995) ix.

[2] United States Naval Institute, retrieved on March 16, 2006, http://www.usni.org/welcome.htm.

[3] United States Naval Institute, retrieved on March 16, 2006, http://www.usni.org/press/press.html.

a great reputation for publishing exceptional narratives from the men and women who protect our country everyday, and one of those women was Dorothy Danner. Even though Danner's autobiography was published by such a distinguished publisher, there are no reviews of *What a Way to Spend a War* in any academic journals.[4]

Based on a close examination of the text, Dorothy Danner's autobiography was written for Americans interested in World War II and the experiences of POWs, especially those of female POWs. Danner definitely wrote her story and the story of the other POWs she was with in internment so that future generations would know what happened to them and learn from their experiences.

The Author

Dorothy Danner was born in 1914 in California, where she was born into a lower middle class family. Danner's family could not afford to send her to nursing school so she became a "probie" student nurse at the Los Angeles General County Hospital. She took a three year course and finally graduated and became a Registered Nurse. Danner worked in two different hospitals until she saw an article in the *American Journal of Nursing*, which contained applications for both the Army and the Navy Nursing Corps. Thinking that it was probably a long shot and that she would never be accepted to either of the nursing programs, especially the Navy since at this time there were only 400 Navy nurses total.[5] Discouraged and not expecting anything to come of her application, Danner sent it in anyway to the Navy, and to her surprise and delight she received an acceptance letter.

When Danner received her acceptance letter from the Navy's Bureau of Medicine and Surgery, she could not have been more excited. She easily passed all of physical and other examinations, and was therefore sent on her first two year tour of duty in 1938 and 1939. Her first orders were close to

---

[4] Online searches in MLA Index and America History & Life yielded no reviews or matches. Book Review Digest did not have any matches either. Also, a general online search of search engines such as www.google.com did not return any responses that were particularly pertinent or informative with the keywords "Dorothy Danner" or "*What a Way to Spend a War*," except for one. There were also no successful searches of major newspapers throughout the country or in Danner's current hometown of Boise, Idaho.

[5] A majority of the biographical information about Dorothy Danner was taken from *What a Way to Spend a War*, but some other information was gathered from the following website. It was the only online source relevant to Danner's life. Oral Histories—U.S. Navy Nurse Prisoner of War in the Philippines, 1942–1945, retrieved on April 10, 2006, http://www.history.navy.mil/faqs/faq87-3f.htm.

Dorothy Danner: What a Way to Spend a War

home in San Diego, California, but soon she received new orders to report to active duty at the U.S. Naval Hospital in Canacao, Philippine Islands.

With these orders Danner was off to new and exciting experiences at every corner. Danner first went to Canacao, then to Manila, where she and the other Navy Nurses and Naval Personnel were made POWs for the first time. The POWs were transported from Manila and brought to Santo Tomas and then later Los Banos, where after four years she was finally rescued from internment by American troops. Soon after her rescue, Danner was made a Lieutenant in the Navy. She came back home to the United States and was reunited with her family. After she recovered from beriberi, which she contracted while in internment, she traveled with the United States Navy in support of the public relations activities. In 1947, Danner left the Navy and was married and had three children and was the grandmother of six. After her death in 2001 she was buried at Arlington National Cemetery.

Framing the Narrative

What a Way to Spend the War does have a dust jacket designed by Karen L. White with a picture of the Navy nurses during their internment at Santo Tomas that is also used within the book. White also added barbed wire around the entire book to enhance the feeling of captivity. On the inside cover of the dust jacket the publisher briefly outlines Danner and the other Navy nurse's internment, and also states the fact that the nurses and the other internees were scheduled for execution on the very day of their rescue by the Eleventh Airborne Division on February 23, 1945. The publisher also discusses the trials and tribulations that the Navy nurses had to endure, but comments that they got through them all with determination and toughness. Also the publisher includes that upon returning home to the United States most of the internees were faced with a lot of other problems that they had to overcome, as well. On the back inside cover of the dust jacket there is a photograph of an aged Danner and a very short biography of her life. The back of the dust jacket is of Danner and the other Navy nurses with Admiral Thomas C. Kinkaid after they had been rescued, which helps to bring closure to the end of the narrative.

There is no introduction or preface to the book, but there is an acknowledgements page and a prologue to introduce the book to the reader. The acknowledgements page gives credit to the other people who helped Danner put together her autobiography, though she did write the narrative by herself. Danner protects the names of those who were POWs with her by changing their names throughout the autobiography, except for the Japanese, some of those in the public domain, and her own. She states that she used the diaries and accounts of internment of several different Doctors, who were POWs with her. Danner also says that she used a well-known journal kept by Medical Records Pharmacist's Mate 2c Robert Kentner.[6] She noted that he kept a daily log because he was ordered to by the Japanese, but that he was also secretly doing it with the intentions of keeping an account for himself for the future after his internment was over. After the acknowledgements page, Danner also included a Prologue before the start of her autobiography. The Prologue was the description of what happened right before the POWs were about to be rescued from internment.

The author provided a dedication before in the beginning of the book. Danner said that her autobiography was "Dedicated to those who were there, *Non intendo facere offensionum.*"[7] Her dedication to her fellow POWs only helps to further prove that Danner wrote this autobiography to show her readers the importance of their POW story during World War II. She was not politically or financially motivated when writing her account. Any reader of *What a Way to Spend a War* can tell through Danner's writing that she was sincere in all that she wrote about and that she truly wanted the world to know about their internment. Even though it took Danner nearly half a century to write their story, she knew that she had to in order to remember their time together and the hardships they faced and eventually overcame.

In between the pages of 104 and 105 Danner included twelve pictures to give the reader a sense of who she was and the conditions of the internment camps. The first picture is a photograph of Danner in 1935, when she was a student at the Los Angeles General County Hospital. Then there was a picture of her standing outside next to the San Diego Naval Hospital during her first tour of duty. Next there are four photographs of and around the Canacao Naval Hospital compound. After this Danner provided a picture of all the Navy nurses interned at Santo Tomas, including the author herself. Then there is a picture of a nurse taking care of a patient, and then of internees washing themselves in a bathtub. Next there are two pictures of liberation from Los Banos, one of all the Navy nurses being briefed by an Admiral, and the second of Danner being interviewed afterward in Guam. The final picture is of Dorothy Danner in 1945 after she had been

---

[6] The original copy of Kentner's Journal can be found through the Washington: Historical Unit, U.S. Army Medical Service, Fort Glen Section, Walter Reed Army Medical Center. The Journal itself was not used for this study.

[7] Danner, Dedication page, "I do not intend to give offense."

Dorothy Danner: What a Way to Spend a War

made a Lieutenant. All of these photographs provide a great portrait of who Danner was, and what life was like as in internee to the Japanese.

Structure of the Narrative

What a Way to Spend a War is a chronological account of Dorothy Danner's life beginning at the point when she decided to become a nurse. Her autobiography starts when she was eighteen years old, and she had high hopes of becoming a costume designer for the Warner Brothers Studios, but her parents had other plans for their daughter. Her parents could not afford the tuition at a nursing school, but they knew that this was a good profession for young Danner because they knew that it would open up a world of opportunities for her. With her parent's encouragement, Dorothy Danner registered as a "probie" at the Los Angeles General County Hospital. She received a small amount of money during her three year course work here, and although this experience did not pay her much money, it did pay her in the lessons and knowledge she gained, because she was taught everything through first hand experience. The autobiography then continues to move chronologically through her enlistment, her orders to become a Navy nurse, her service to her country, and her time spent as a POW. Danner's narrative ends with her liberation from her internment camp in the Philippines. She returns home to her family in California. Shortly after this she is made a Lieutenant in the Navy. The last line of the narrative was from a telephone call that she received from one of the other internee's many years after their rescue. It was from Mitch, another POW whom with she had a very personal relationship with while in internment. The call was a reminder of the past, with Mitch telling her, "I don't care what your old man says, doll, I love you."[8] Their relationship had never been anything more than friendship as far as Danner lets on, because Mitch was married during their internment, and Danner herself married later, but this phone call was from a long lost love that she never got to end things with in the way that she would have liked. Most importantly though, Danner probably includes this telephone call to show that she did not have much closure from her time as a POW, and that she may have been experiencing some sort of Post Traumatic Stress that she had not yet dealt with. Danner may have chose to do this in such a subtle manner because she never expresses her internment as anything too terrible, but maybe she did not give her readers the full story, and it is their responsibility to see past her omissions.

[8] Ibid., 215.

Throughout Danner's account of her experience in World War II every scene and chapter of the book flows easily into the next. There are no flashbacks or dreams that get in the way of the author's chronological account. At some moments Danner discussed thinking about people from her past, but she only talked about them in reference to the time that she was thinking about them during her internment.

The genre of *What a Way to Spend a War* is a survivor narrative. Danner wrote the autobiography in order to honor the lives and experiences of the POWS that she served with throughout her time in internment. Although Danner changed the names of many of people she was a POW with, she honors them enough by just telling their stories to the world in a respectful manner.

Construction of the Narrative

The way in which Danner constructed her narrative made the autobiography very easy to read and follow. She wrote this text in a way that was very plain and direct. Danner does not include any complicated images or metaphors, which some other authors use that can often confuse the reader. Instead, the entire autobiography was very simply stated. Her writing style was definitely constructed to suit most audiences because of the straightforward nature of the text. Danner does not footnote or mention any other texts by name throughout the narrative, although in her acknowledgements page before she began the text, she stated that she did use other references to help jog her own memory and add more detail to her own autobiography.

Contents of the Narrative

The first chapter of *What a Way to Spend a War* is "Becoming a Nurse." In this chapter the author describes her life before she enlisted in the military. The author included this information in the narrative to show how important it was for her to become a Navy nurse at this time, and how excited she was to embark on this new journey in her life. Danner thought of the opportunity to serve as a Navy nurse to be a great honor and she could not have been happier with the opportunity to serve her country.[9]

The next two chapters focus on her initial feelings about her call to active duty. These chapters are called "Arrival in Fantasyland" and "Happy Days." Danner discusses leaving San Francisco Bay upon the *Henderson* and arriving in Canacao Bay. She does not say one bad thing about her

---

[9] Ibid., 3–6.

Dorothy Danner: What a Way to Spend a War

first impression of the Canacao Bay Naval Hospital. Danner mentions exceptional nurse's quarters, lavish parties, the necessity of formal and party dresses, and all of the history around her, which completely blew her away and made her extremely excited about her first tour of active duty. Also, she included the fact that they had maids to clean up after them and press their clothing, which was something that she was definitely not expecting to have happen while she was serving her country, and it was especially a change for someone from her lower class background. She included this section of the autobiography to show how good she and the other Navy nurses had it before they became POWs.[10] Also, up until this point in the narrative Danner was explaining an adventurous time in her life, but soon her adventure would change into a nightmare.

Throughout these initial chapters Danner also dedicates a lot of stories and information about meeting the young Ensign Johnny Osbourne. Danner seemed to fall instantly in love with him, but she soon learned that it was too good to be true. Johnny was a playboy, and he did not really seem to be interested in Danner the way she was with him. Danner was forced to realize that Johnny was not looking to get serious with her and she began to curse his name and constantly obsess over their relationship. She received a letter from him, which only infuriated her more, so she wrote him back to him, "YOU AND YOUR DAMNED HOUSTON CAN GO TO HELL!"[11] This statement alone would traumatize and eat away at Danner for her entire service and internment, because shortly after she responded hostilities with the Japanese were getting worse, and they bombed Pearl Harbor. This severely hurt Danner and her infatuation and infatuation with Johnny did not end at the "fantasyland" of Canacao Bay, rather it carried on throughout the rest of the narrative and constantly traumatized Danner to her very core.

Danner's world was turned upside down when the Japanese began to become a greater threat to the United States, and there was a lot of hysteria around the Naval Hospital. But then all of sudden the Japanese bombed Pearl Harbor, and thus the fourth chapter of the book "Pearl Harbor." With America under attack all that Dorothy Danner could think of was getting back the letter that she sent out to Johnny, because she did not want to have cursed him or the *Houston*, especially with all of these terrible things happening all around the world.

---

[10] Ibid., 7–24.
[11] Ibid., 29. All capital letters were used in Danner's original autobiography.

Danner included the next couple of chapters in the narrative to show how now her "fantasyland was lifeless and stripped."[12] She goes into great depth describing all of the casualties and lack of supplies to take care of those who were not killed during the attacks. Danner then discussed transporting the patients to Manila via boat with the other Navy nurses. At Manila, she was able to contact her family with a telegraph saying that amidst all of the chaos that she was alright and that they should not worry about her.

Danner, though, was not really safe as she told her family she was because there were many bombers still flying overhead, and soon Manila was declared an open city. Almost immediately after this the Navy and Army nurses, along with their patients received the news that the Japanese had sent out a proclamation, and they all were now Japanese POWs. Danner described their initial occupation as pretty decent, but this all deteriorated and the Japanese began to get more violent, and they soon sent the POWs to the Santo Tomas Internment Camp.

From the tenth to the twenty-second chapter Danner gave a detailed description of her and the other internee's time spent as POWs. During this time Danner went through many life changing moments. She became a Catholic on Easter Sunday, because after watching the comfort and relief the Catholic nurses got from praying, she too wanted to feel that way. Also, she had yet to overcome all of the guilt and regret she was feeling about the letter she had written to Johnny, and her conversion helped her to deal with all of this. Danner hoped and prayed everyday that she had not wished him such a terrible fate. Her conversion to Christianity was a very fundamental aspect of her entire internment because it gave her the faith she needed to get through her rough experience as a POW, even though she does not always express how terrible it actually was at times.

After being at Santo Tomas for a while, Danner and the other Navy nurses were sent to work at Los Banos, another internment camp. They had to set up a hospital here to take care of all the injured internees, and they were paid by the Japanese government. Danner's internment was very unusual in that she was paid to work in the hospital. This made Danner and the other Navy nurses very valuable to the Japanese, and because of this the Japanese seemed to have some degree of respect for the American women. The Japanese knew that the nurses were a resource that they could not exploit. This was probably why Danner's internment does not seem to have been as awful as it could have been, or that it was for more expendable internees in the eyes of their Japanese captors. This was especially the case

---

[12] Ibid., 53.

because Danner does not tell any stories of rapes or of any battering to herself or any of the other Navy nurses while they were POWs. The potential hardships that Danner could have experienced were minimized because she worked for the Japanese, but this did not mean that it minimized her heartache or the psychological distress that she would later face upon returning home to the United States.[13]

Unlike other POW accounts Dorothy Danner goes into great deal about all of her relationships with the other people that she encounterd during her service and internment. There are two relationships in general that she goes into great detail about, one was her relationship with Johnny, and the other was with a man named Mitch, who she was an internee with for a great deal of time. Other POWs with a hidden agenda, such as running for political office, would not have included these relationships in their narratives. Danner though, having no other motives other than to tell her story included these intimate relationships to show the effects of internment and how they made people desperate for some sort of intimate relationship, even if it was completely platonic.

Danner's relationship with Johnny plagued her entire experience in World War II starting with the bombing of Pearl Harbor all the way up to her rescue from Los Banos. She never seemed to be able to shake his memory, or stop wondering what was going on with him, or if he was even alive. As for Mitch though, he was a married man, who she had a very intimate relationship with, and although she never mentions any sexual aspect of the relationship, the other internees and Catholic priests in the camp made her feel bad about their friendship.[14] The relationship though between Dorothy and Mitch was very important for both of them because they became each others strength in pushing through all of the tough days, especially when they were not sure if they were going to live long enough to make it out of the camp or if that particular day was the day that the Japanese were going to kill them all. Danner has no shame in showing that she had somewhat romantic feelings during her POW experience; most men, and even women, who were POWs would have never vocalized their affection for another person in this manner. By including these details, Danner shows that she was not afraid of expressing all of her true feelings, and this shows that Danner's account was truly genuine and factual.

---

[13] Ibid., 124–92.

[14] Danner would probably have never engaged in such a close relationship with a married man had she never become a POW. The circumstances she was in caused her to look for camaraderie wherever she could find it.

The garden at Los Banos was one of the most significant things in Danner's life during her internment. It helped her to get through the extremely long days; she was able to find solace and strength by tending something greater than herself. Danner included this information about her garden in her autobiography to show that this was the only place during her time of internment that she ever felt like she had any control. Also, Danner found the garden to be calming, which was a great help during a time of much uncertainty. The garden at Los Banos was Danner's spiritual haven, where she found peace during this time of war.

In the last three chapters of Danner's narrative she detailed the account of her rescue, liberation, and return home to the United States. The end of the autobiography really brought the narrative around full circle, since she ended up back at home with her family in California after four years as a POW. Her life after being a POW seemed to be a pretty great part of her life because she was made a Lieutenant in the Navy, which gave her some more respect amongst her peers. Even though she was honored with this title, the author does not make a big deal about her new position, which further shows the honesty of her POW account and her hopes of simply telling her story with no other strings attached.

Conclusion

In conclusion, Dorothy Danner's autobiography *What a Way to Spend a War* is an extremely interesting narrative that is unlike all others in that the author goes into detail and discusses situations and events that other POWs would not have included. Also, Danner's treatment in internment was unique because she did not receive the harsh treatment that many other POWs have experienced because she was valuable to the Japanese. Danner was an extremely strong woman and her strength and intellect shine through her insightful internment memoir.

William F. Dean:
General Dean's Story

A Korean War Memoir

SARAH BURKE

The Text

GENERAL DEAN'S Story: As Told to William L. Worden by Major General William F. Dean was published by the Viking Press, in 1954. *General Dean's Story* was also serialized in the *Saturday Evening Post* in 1954 under the title, "My Three Years as a Dead Man," written by William L. Worden. Worden wrote a number of other stories for the *Saturday Evening Post* such as, "A Room for a Soldier" (1944), "The Cruelest Weapon in Korea" (1951), and "Cold War in the Formosa Strait" (1955). General Dean also employed the assistance of William L. Worden in preparing this manuscript.

General Dean's Story was reviewed in the *New York Times* in May of 1954.[1] There were no references to *General Dean's Story* in the MLA Index or America History and Life.[2] After completing the text it is apparent that the general audience intended is those who wanted to hear the complete story of his much publicized capture and release. It is also made extremely clear that General Dean did not consider himself a hero. He states, ". . . when I think about the men who did better jobs—some who died doing them . . . I wouldn't have awarded myself a wooden star for what I did as a commander."[3] It can hardly be doubted that a highly ranking officer, who was captured because he got lost from his own command, felt the need to explain his actions.

---

[1] The *New York Times* (May 7, 1954), 21.
[2] MLA searched 03/20/06; AH&L searched 03/20/06.
[3] William F. Dean, *General Dean's Story* (New York: Viking, 1954), 3.

The Author

William F. Dean (1899–1981) was born in Carlyle, Illinois. Growing up he had always loved the army, but due to his age he was unable to fight in WWI.[4] He was rejected from West Point, so he joined the Students' Army Training Corps at the University of California, where he planned to study pre-law. Dean never received a degree, but he did secure a regular commission as a second lieutenant on October 18, 1923, where he was assigned to the 38th Infantry Regiment at Fort Douglas, Utah. It was during this time that Dean married Mildred Dern, whom he had two children with. He reached lieutenant in twelve years followed by captain in 1936 and major in 1940.

Dean finally received the opportunity to go to war in 1943. He was commander of the 44th Infantry Division in Europe. Due to his exceptional service during that campaign he was awarded the Distinguished Service Cross for Bravery. In October of 1947 he became the military governor in South Korea. In 1948 he took command of the 7th Infantry Division which was stationed in Japan. He then served as the 8th U.S. Army Chief of Staff. Following this he was promoted to Major General and took command of the 24th Infantry Division, which were headquartered in Kokura on the southern Japanese island of Kyushu, in October 1949.

Framing of the Narrative

General Dean's Story did contain a dust jacket that had a picture of General Dean on the front and a picture of him at Freedom Village on the day of his release on the back. The back also contained a citation, which accompanied his reception of the Congressional Medal of Honor. The inside flap of the dust jacket contained some information about the book, but it mainly commended him for his ability to survive his internment. It also endorsed a number of other contemporary works, which were published by Viking Press.

There is a collaborator's note by William L. Worden, which discussed his experience and perceptions of Dean. Worden stated that " . . . General Dean wrote the book himself by speaking it. Not only are the facts his own, without additions from me, but the language is his own."[5] Worden also stated that they only disagreed on one issue, which was the fact that Dean did *not* consider himself a true hero or a great commander. The text also had an introduction written by Dean, which was very unusual. Unlike

---

[4] Biographical information is drawn from *General Dean's Story*, 6.
[5] Worden, Collaborator's Note, ix.

William F. Dean: General Dean's Story

other generals' autobiographies, Dean admits to his mistakes and praises others over himself. The book also contains a Korean War chronology and an index. There is a map and multiple pictures, which greatly enhanced the book because they helped to legitimize his story. General Dean dedicated the book "to the many friends who for three long years never gave up hope."[6]

Structure of the Narrative

The first chapter of General Dean's story begins with his birth and then briefly describes his life up to his departure for Korea on July 3, 1950. The second chapter deals with his missions in Korea. Dean was mainly in charge of leading tank killer missions. During this section of the book he is extremely descriptive of some of the killings he saw. For example, "He said Colonel Martin had grabbed a 2.6 bazooka and was leading his men with it . . . when one tank came around a corner unexpectedly and fired from less than 25 feet. The shot blew Colonel Martin in half."[7] The third chapter describes in detail the mission that Dean led, where he directed a caravan of jeeps down a wrong road where they were ambushed. It goes on to explain how the rest of the men were able to escape, but Dean was separated. He was extremely injured with a dislocated shoulder and no supplies. Dean hid in the mountains for thirty-five days, where he received help from various families. Dean was eventually befriended by a young boy named Han, whom he thought was helping him but he actually led Dean into a trap.[8] Dean was captured on August 25, 1950, which was his wedding anniversary. Dean spent 1,105 days in captivity where he was interrogated, but never tortured. During his captivity, Dean did attempt suicide but was unsuccessful because the gun malfunctioned.[8] The text concludes with his release on September 4, 1953. General Dean was the highest ranking prisoner of war in the conflict.

The text is chronological and mainly a single constructed perspective. The major turning point occurs in chapter eleven. General Dean had had no contact with the outside until he was interviewed on December 18, 1951 by an Australian, Wilfred Burchett who was a correspondent for Le Soir, a French left-wing newspaper. This was the first instance that anyone had any idea General Dean was alive since being reported missing in ac-

---

[6] Dean, Dedication.
[7] Ibid., 25.
[8] Ibid., trap, 80; gun, 159.

tion. This was considered a turning point because it is the first indication that the end to his captivity was near.[9]

Construction of the Narrative

The style of *General Dean's Story* is plain and direct therefore the sentences are simple and declarative. It appears that this story was not modeled after any previous text. It is obvious that Dean's main motivation for writing this memoir is to provide an explanation for his capture. The largest section of the text dealt with his captivity. His experience was not described as intolerable because he was a high ranking officer, so he was treated very well, which is probably why he never demonizes his captors. The only major problem during his captivity was a terrible case of dysentery. Therefore the theme of this text is one of adventure and illness.

Contents of the Narrative

It is very apparent from the beginning of the text that Dean loved all aspects of military life. He loved it so much that at fifteen he wanted to enlist in the army and fight in WWI, but his mother refused to grant him permission. Throughout the text Dean conveyed himself as very humble and moral. This is demonstrated earlier in the text when he stated "Part of the job is to send men into places from which you know they are not likely to come out again . . . it's an especially soul-searing business when the only thing you can buy with other men's lives is a little more time."[10] It is due to these character traits that when Dean is captured he is extremely angry, but mainly humbled and embarrassed. He never blamed anyone but himself. At one point Dean stated to his captors, "You have to remember that all American Generals are not as dumb as I am. You just happened to catch the dumbest."[11] Dean continued to act in this manner until the very end. Upon his release, instead of being released first because of his rank, he decided to wait until his name was called just like every other newly released soldier. Even though Dean did not seem to think that he deserved a Congressional Medal of Honor[12] it is very apparent that he absolutely did because he was able to maintain composure under extreme pressure.[13]

---

[9] Ibid., interview, 238–243.
[10] Ibid., 30.
[11] Ibid., 145.
[12] Ibid., 3.
[13] Ibid., 137–154.

William F. Dean: General Dean's Story
Conclusion

To my reading the main purpose for writing this memoir was to provide an explanation for his capture. Due to this, *General Dean's Story* is not like the typical American POW autobiography. At no point during his memoir does General Dean blame anyone for his capture but himself. This is extremely unusual because in most POW accounts there are many excuses to show that the soldier's capture was not his fault. By approaching his story in this manner Dean was able to clearly convey to the readers his humbling experiences as a POW during the Korean War, and to make his case that his capture was the result of simple incompetence and bad luck—not the result of something sinister.[14]

---

[14] General Dean's memoir, published during the Army McCarthy Hearings April–June 1954 to deal with Senator McCarthy's charges of Communist infiltration of the Army, may have been, in part, a response to allegations that were in the air at this time.

Jeremiah Denton:
When Hell Was in Session

A Vietnam Memoir

SEAN WHALEN

The Text

WHEN HELL *Was in Session* written by Jeremiah Denton was published by the Readers Digest Press in 1976. Denton acknowledges that he was helped in writing this book by Ed Brandt. Ed Brandt is a native of Baltimore, where he graduated from Baltimore City College. He also attended Western Maryland College. In 1950 he joined the staff of the *Baltimore Sun*, and was then a Metropolitan Editor of the Norfolk Virginia *Virginian Pilot.* He is also the author of *The Last Voyage of USS Pueblo*.[1] I was able to find two reviews of *When Hell Was in Session*, after searching the America History and Life Index. I also searched the MLA Index but there was no information regarding the book. It is my opinion Denton's POW account was written to inform the public about his experience as a prisoner of war in Vietnam, to show that he was not broken by internment and to encourage other POWs.

The Author

Jeremiah Denton was born July 15, 1924, in Mobile, Alabama. Denton attended the McGill Institute, and then Spring Hill College. He then went on to graduate from the United States Naval Academy in 1946.[2] Denton served in the navy from 1946 to 1977. Denton was a prisoner of

---

[1] Denton, *When Hell Was in Session*, dust jacket.

[2] Denton, dust jacket. I assume this is the same Ed Brandt who is mentioned on page 211 as the journalist who assisted the POWs' wives in publicizing the mistreatment of the POWs.

war from 1965 to 1973. After returning home Denton served for three more years before retiring with a rank of rear admiral. In 1980, Denton ran as a Republican for a U.S. Senate seat from his home state of Alabama and achieved a victory over Democrat James E. Folsom Jr. In the Senate, he compiled a solidly conservative, pro-life and pro-national security voting record. In 1986, he narrowly lost his bid for re-election to Richard C. Shelby, who was then a Democrat.

Framing of the Narrative

When Hell Was in Session has a dust jacket with a picture of Denton in prison on the front cover along with the title of the book and author's name. The back of the dust jacket has a picture of Denton returning home and being reunited with his wife. Inside of the jacket there is a paragraph describing one moment of Denton's experience as a POW and also a small paragraph with some information on his life. There is a four-page preface before the book starts that gives some basic information about the prison camp experience including a chart that describes the tap code that was developed by soldiers inside the Hanoi Hilton. The memoir contains some devotional poetry written by Denton while he was a POW, a letter Denton's wife received from President Lyndon Johnson, excerpts of a captured document that described American POWs, a quotation of a maxim of William Penn, and sections of the Code of Conduct with a brief commentary by Denton.[3] At the end of the account there is a short epilogue detailing Denton's return home. The book is dedicated to "Those who strive to make this one nation under God, who are willing to sacrifice to protect her, who thank God for such great beauty as she has developed, and who patiently tolerate her imperfections." The pictures on the jacket suggest that the author has passed through an intense experience of internment back into everyday American life.

Structure of the Narrative

When Hell Was in Session starts in Denton's preparation for the mission where he is shot down. The first paragraph of the second chapter describes Denton's life before he was shot down, and then the rest of the memoir is written in chronological order. I would say that the turning point for this book is in the first chapter when Denton is shot down and becomes a POW. The rest of the account is about his time in prison; however, in

---

[3] Denton, 163–64, 186–87 (poetry), 101–02 (letter), 98–100 (document), 239 (Penn), 46–49 (Code).

describing his POW experience Denton also describes how this experience deepened his religious faith.[4]

Construction of the Narrative

The style of *When Hell Was in Session* is very plain. This account is written with no metaphors or literary quotes. The twenty short chapters are numbered, but not given titles.[5] The sentences are simple and describe what happened in the prison camp. The narrative makes extensive use of dialogue. There are not many flashbacks and few other details of Denton's life are included, but there are several shifts of locale between Denton's cell in Vietnam and his family in Virginia Beach, Virginia.[6] A basic theme of this account is Denton's anger for the way that he was treated during his time as a prisoner. At the end of the first chapter Denton recalls: "Dazed and bleeding as I was, my principal emotion was fury. I was mad as hell at being shot down, and even angrier at being captured."[7] Denton's self construction is as a devoted fighting man who fears dishonor more than pain.[8]

The Contents of the Narrative

Jeremiah Denton was taken as a prisoner of war by the North Vietnamese on July 18, 1965 after his plane was shot down on a bombing mission. When his plane was shot down he snapped a tendon in his left thigh and his leg became useless.[9] Denton received minimal treatment for this injury as a POW, but he does note several acts of kindness extended toward him by ordinary Vietnamese because of his injuries and internment.[10] After his capture he was blindfolded and taken as a prisoner to the Hoa Lo Prison

---

[4] Ibid., 66, 84, 15, 163, 187, 221.

[5] The longest chapter, sixteen, is twenty-two and a half pages; the two shortest chapters, three and five are five pages; the average chapter length is eleven pages. There is no table of contents, but there is an index.

[6] Ibid., 20–22, 68, 96, 208–14. The seminar instructor wondered if the street address Denton gave for his family, Watergate Lane, was symbolic, but he informs me that after some research he determined that there is a Watergate Lane in Virginia Beach.

[7] Ibid., 10.

[8] Ibid., 32, 84.

[9] Ibid., 5–6. Denton's description of his injury was submitted to an orthopedic surgeon for comment. The surgeon suggested that a more likely medical description of Denton's injury was a sudden rupture of the Achilles tendon. Letter from Dr. Yousaf Ali M.D., Rheumatology Associates, March 29, 2006. It is unlikely that the tendon could have in Denton's words, "recoiled and curled up into my abdomen," but it may have felt like that.

[10] Ibid., 15, 136, 144, 189.

or as the Americans called it the "Hanoi Hilton" and was kept there until February 12, 1973.[11] During his time there he was kept in solitary confinement in a cell that was nine-feet-by-eight-feet, starved and tortured.[12] In the cell were two concrete beds, with metal and wood stocks at the foot of each one and there was a small bucket which was used as a toilet. The door to the cell had a peephole and there were windows that were covered by a thin layer of concrete. While in prison Denton was frequently questioned about his family and personal life, but he would never give any information up due to the code of conduct that he was taught by the navy. The only answer that Denton would answer without being tortured was his name, rank, service number, and birth date.[13] The soldiers in the prison set up a chain of command based on rank and were able to communicate by tapping on walls. This was very important for all of them because it was the only form of communication that they had with other people besides the interrogators. Denton reveals that in the early stages of his imprisonment that he was tortured by the thought of being broken by the Vietnamese and giving up information. To get away from these thoughts he came up with a daily routine which consisted of prayer, exercise, escape plans, eat, nap, communicate with other prisoners, and then start the cycle again.[14]

Denton's first experience with torture came during a cell inspection when the guards noticed that he had broken the window frame in his cell.[15] He was locked up in the stocks in his cell, which led to an infection in his foot due to cuts from the rusted iron stocks. His rations were reduced and he decided to stop eating all together. When the guards brought him back to the full rations he still would not eat. His infection led to periods of high fever and delirium. He finally gave a false answer to one of the questions that was asked to him and he was let out of the stocks. In November of 1965 the rations were cut down to one bowl of soup per day and for some prisoners it was dropped to one piece of bread and a cup of water. Denton dropped from 167 pounds to 120 pounds in those first few months.[16] The most effective way of torture the Vietnamese used was tying the prisoners

---

[11] Denton mentions several nicknames for the guards (mainly animal names such as Cat, Dog, Rat, and Pigeye, but there are other names such as Gunga Din, Teenager, and Smiley) and for locations (such as Alcatraz, Stardust, Little Vegas, and Mint).

[12] Denton, 28. Denton mentions six major torture sessions (132), and he notes "Strangely, they never did torture me to obtain credible military information . . . " (29).

[13] Ibid., 30.

[14] Ibid., 40.

[15] Ibid., 41.

[16] Ibid., 56.

arms behind them from the elbows to the shoulders with the ropes pulled as tightly as possible.[17] This method was used frequently and had a very high success rate. Denton had to go through this several times and every time he would give meaningless answers to questions to get free. Maybe Denton's most memorable moment was when he was taken for a television interview that was aired around the world. During the interview Denton continuously blinked out the word torture.[18] Because of this performance Denton's hands were handcuffed behind his back and connected to his ankles. During this torture Denton questioned whether he would be able to keep his sanity. When he was let free he wrote a 36 page paper on how he had bombed churches and neighborhoods several times. Another example of the humiliation he was put through was a march that he had to take along with other prisoners through the streets of Hanoi. They were handcuffed together while the crowd beat them for every step of the march.[19] Denton went through one five-day torture session in which he gave no information and he was released by defeated guards, but because of this he was kept in isolation.

In the spring of 1967 Denton and eleven other prisoners were taken to another prison. The prison was called Alcatraz and Denton was held there for two years.[20] Once again Denton was put in solitary confinement, in a cell that was 47 square inches, with a pallet to sleep on and no window.[21] Every prisoner there went through incredible amounts of torture and none of them ever broke down or gave away information easily. He was returned to Hanoi Hilton in 1969 to a bigger cell and he was finally given a cell mate. After this conditions continued to improve and he was kept in prison until February 12, 1973 when he was released. When he returned to America he was invited to make the first comments on arrival. Denton's final comments of the book are "We are profoundly grateful to our commander in chief and to our nation for this day. God bless America!"[22]

Conclusion

I think that there were a few objectives in this narrative. The first was to show that even though Denton faced a lot of adversity he was never broken

---

[17] Ibid., 58.
[18] Ibid., 91.
[19] Ibid., 110.
[20] Ibid., 147.
[21] Ibid., 147.
[22] Ibid., 235.

down completely by the enemy. I think that he might have written this as a model for other potential soldiers who will become prisoners of war. Denton never gave up information and he acted like a leader the whole time he was imprisoned. Another reason he wrote this was just to tell the world his story of the war, and to show that his war with his captors was heroic even though he did not get to fight in most of the war because he was a POW.

John McCain:
Faith of My Fathers

A Vietnam War Memoir

Pete Farese

The Text

Faith of My Fathers by John McCain was published in 1999 by Random House, New York. This is the only publication of this book and was written by McCain with help from his future chief of staff, Mark Salter.

There were two notable reviews that I have found especially helpful when reading this text: "Hero of the Hanoi Hilton" by Nathaniel Tripp, and the other "Standing Humbly Before a Noble Family Tradition" by Richard Bernstein. Tripp describes John McCain "as a strong-willed maverick . . . prepared to be the prisoner from hell . . . [with] not only the strength to survive, but a renewed determination to serve his country."[1] Bernstein looks at McCain in a different light, referring to him as a, "model of modesty, honorable, and courageous . . . [inspired] by his father, grandfather, and the amazing spirit of resistance demonstrated by the other Americans held in Hanoi."[2] Both reviewers note that McCain is restrained in telling much detail about his imprisonment, leaving the reader, "looking for deeper insights."[3] The book had a detailed description of his family history and imprisonment, yet John McCain still manages to leave much to the imagination.[4]

---

[1] "Heroes of the Hanoi Hilton" by Nathaniel Tripp, *New York Times*, 3 October 1999, Book Review, 17.
[2] "Standing Humbly Before a Noble Family Tradition" by Richard Bernstein, *New York Times*, 1 October 1999, E, 45.
[3] Tripp, "Heroes."
[4] When searching through America: History and Life as well as the MLA Index, there were

The Author

John Sidney McCain was born on 29 August 1936 in Coco Solo in the U.S. Controlled Panama Canal Zone.[5] He attended Episcopal High School in Alexandria, VA, graduated in 1954 and went on to the United States Naval Academy where both his father and grandfather, two prominent four-star admirals, had attended. He was a midshipman for 4 years at the Academy and graduated 894 out of 899. He went on to become a Captain and a Naval Airman.[6] The book does not describe John McCain's life after the military; however, he does go on to become a prominent Republican Senator for Arizona. Also, there is an extensive family history, which indicates that McCain is a descendant of the medieval Emperor Charlemagne.[7]

Framing the Narrative

The dust jacket and the third page of the book contain three important pictures that were also spread throughout the chapters of the book. One of John McCain Sr., one of John McCain Jr. and Sr. meeting on a ship prior to the death of John McCain Sr., and the final picture was of John Sidney McCain in his Airman uniform standing next to his plane. On the inside flaps of the dust jacket there is a short description of the book, along with two reviews, one from *Publishers Weekly* and the other from *Library Journal*. On the rear inside flap, there is a quick "About the Authors" section describing briefly both John McCain and Mark Salter.[8] On the rear of the dust cover are three more reviews, one from William J. Bennett, another from the *Kirkus Reviews,* and the third from General Colin L. Powell (ret).

There is a short, two-paged preface in which McCain gives much of the credit for writing the book to the inspiration of both his father and grandfather. The following acknowledgements section is a display of gratitude towards many of the people who had influenced McCain during his young career, his imprisonment, as well as his friends and wives who

---

no hits for the title in either. The searches were conducted on both 27 March 2006, as well as 6 April 2006 to no avail.

[5] John McCain with Mark Salter, *Faith of My Fathers* (New York: Random House, 1999), 47, hereafter cited as McCain.

[6] McCain, 108–52.

[7] McCain, 20, John McCain with Mark Salter, *Worth The Fighting For: A Memoir* (New York: Random House, 2002) describes McCain's subsequent career.

[8] This is reprinted at the end of the book on an unnumbered page that would be 351.

had helped him and Mark Salter write the book. The book is dedicated to Doug, Andy, Sidney, Meghan, Jack, Jimmy, and Bridget.[9]

Faith of My Fathers is divided into three sections. Prior to Chapter one and the beginning of the first section there is an excerpt from the hymn, "Faith of Our Fathers" by Frederick William Faber.[10] At the beginning of the second section, on page 97 before chapter nine, there is an excerpt from William Butler Yeats' poem, "The Old Men Admiring Themselves in Water."[11] Finally, at the beginning of the third section, on page 175 before chapter fourteen there is an excerpt from Alfred Lord Tennyson's poem, "Lancelot and Elaine."[12] What is quite particular about these quotes is that none of them seem to be about the leadership McCain tries to depict of himself throughout his years in the military. Each quote seems to be based on the principles of being a good "follower," perhaps in an attempt to show how he is following in his father's and grandfather's footsteps. Yet, the role of any officer within the United States Military of which John McCain was a member is to know, understand, and display the virtue of leadership.

Structure of the Narrative

The narrative is constructed so that the first third of the book is focused on John McCain's father and grandfather; and the two thirds is a description of McCain's own actions as a Navy Airman as well as his imprisonment in Hanoi, Vietnam.[13] Beginning with his extensive family tree dating back to Charlemagne, McCain describes in detail his grandfather's life and time in service, then his father's amazing story, and lastly his own, which, in

---

[9] McCain, xi (the author and co-author's children).

[10] Faith of our fathers, living still,
In spite of dungeon, fire and sword;
O How our hearts beat high with joy
Whenever we hear that glorious word!
Faith of our fathers, holy faith!
We will be true to thee till death.

For Frederick Faber (1814–1863) see *The Oxford Dictionary of Christians Church* eds. F.L. Cross and E.A. Livingstone, 3rd ed. (Oxford: Oxford University Press, 1997), 593.

[11] I heard the old, old man say,
'All that's beautiful drifts away
Like the waters.'

[12] In me there dwells
No greatness, save it be some far-off touch,
Of greatness to know well I am not great.

[13] There is a brief shift back to memories of his grandfather in the section entitled *Commander-in-Chief*.

the light of his grandfather and father's stories, seems quite deplorable. He brings us through his rebel years as a child through high school and then into his four years at the United States Naval Academy. Barely passing the Naval Academy, McCain was soon sent to various naval airman schools as well as different ships until he was deployed to the *USS Oriskany*, which was off the coast of Vietnam. The turning point of the book, would have to be when he describes how he was shot down over Vietnam, captured, and imprisoned for over five years. This narrative is basically chronological and told as a string of memories beginning with early life and ending with his release as a POW yet does not go any further into his life after his release. The overall pattern for the first half of the book, which recounts fond memories of his father and grandfather, is like the Passion narratives in the four Gospels. The second half of the book, however, could be compared to the pattern of the Book of Job, where McCain, like Job, is constantly battered and beaten, but never gives up hope and his desire to defend his country and the other American POWs in the camp. It is possible to describe *Faith of My Fathers* as an unassuming conversion account.

Construction of the Narrative

The style of the narrative is basically a string of memories beginning with McCain's fondest memories of his grandfather, both his and his father's relationship with him, and his grandfather's significant accomplishments during his time in service. It goes on to describe his memories of his father, his relationship with him, as well as his father's accomplishments during his time in service. McCain then describes his time in service and compares this to his father and grandfathers'. With the exception of being a POW for over five years, McCain's service record seems meager in comparison with the distinguishable service of his father and grandfather. His deep respect for his predecessors' accomplishments in the Navy in comparison with his own is evident throughout the book. The second half of the book is a lengthy description of his imprisonment in the Hanoi Hilton in Vietnam. Although there were no apparent images used throughout the book, McCain still manages to describe his story with much detail. What seemed interesting is that there was not very much correlation from his father and grandfathers' stories to his imprisonment that could offer any rhyme or reason behind any of his actions. He mentions himself in the Preface that his perseverance was assumed from his parents, but not much else. However, the audience, could be any person who has not had much time in service if any at all. In fact, McCain goes so far as to reiterate US Code of Military Conduct for American Prisoners of War, simply to bring this knowledge to any reader without a military background.[14]

Contents of the Narrative

The first third of *Faith of my Fathers* is nothing more than a chronological series of vignettes as told by memories of McCain as well as long family stories. These described both the services of John McCain Sr. and Jr., with little more about John as a child. Random stories are included such as the memory of drinking whiskey at the age of only seventeen with Admiral William F. Halsey as a new destroyer was commissioned in his grandfather's name.[15] The overall theme, however, is that John McCain had absolutely no intention of joining the service when he was younger. However, once he came close to graduating high school, it became more apparent that he would end up following in his father and grandfathers' footsteps and attend the Naval Academy. He graduated USNA in 1958, 894th out of 899, and was almost kicked out numerous times for poor grades, a bad attitude, and a seemingly insurmountable number of demerits.

The description of his time in the military was tarnished by more stories of drunken debauchery rather than accomplishments. He went to naval flight school in Pensacola, followed by advanced flight training in Corpus Christi, TX. From there his orders were to fly A-1 Skyraiders off of the USS *Enterprise*. After describing a few fond memories of his time on the *Enterprise*, but probably more memories of drunken parties and misconduct, he describes moving to the USS *Forrestal* in 1966, and flying the A-4 Skyhawk. It was here where the *Forrestal* had caught fire and ended up going out of commission. From there, McCain joined the USS *Oriskany* in 1967, as part of Operation Rolling Thunder over Vietnam. It was from here on 26 October 1967, on his 23rd bombing raid where a SAM hit him; a telephone pole-like missile used by the Vietnamese, and blew off his right wing. He went down in enemy territory and was captured. This is the beginning of the POW experience that comprises over two-thirds of this book.[16]

---

[14] *Faith of My Fathers* was published in 1999, shortly before McCain was a candidate for the Republican presidential nomination. This could be a coincidence, but it is also possible that McCain chose to write a memoir as a way of presenting a coherent narrative of his wartime experience before his story was fragmented by election coverage.

[15] McCain, 46.

[16] Ibid., 153–89.

McCain was dragged out of a lake, seeing his knee bent sideways. In severe pain he was brought to Hao Lo, or as the prisoners referred to it, The Hanoi Hilton. McCain bargained with the Vietnamese prison guards that if they gave him medical treatment on his leg, he would give them intelligence, with absolutely no intention of saying a word to them. After weeks of deliberation, he was finally able to spend a few weeks in the hospital for surgery on his knee. Once he returned to Hao Lo, he was placed within a cell with other Americans until he recovered. Here he met two men whom he would never forget. ". . . Bud Day and Norris Overly saved my life."[17] These two men had helped feed him, help him to the toilet/bucket, and even massaged his leg so as to help blood flow. They had stuck together, for the most part through the hard times in the prison, with the exception of Norris, who was offered early release due to family history and his rank. Later, McCain was offered the same, but turned it down, because of his feeling of disloyalty to the other prisoners as well as his country.

After a few months of living with Bud and Norris, John McCain was able to walk on his own and thus was put in his separate cell. It was here, and in the brief moments he would spend together with the other American POWs where McCain describes the prison guards, each one of them having a name: "Bug" was the mean interrogator, "The Cat" was the prison Commandant, "The Rabbit" was a translator/interrogator, etc. Not only guards, but different buildings and places throughout the camp were also given nicknames; "The Gun Shed" where John, Bud, and Norris stayed together, "The Warehouse" a solitary confinement building, "The Plantation" where they were sent towards the end of the war and were given slightly better treatment, etc.[18]

McCain explains that he would often visit "The Warehouse" because he was the epitome of a "prisoner from hell" with what the Vietnamese referred to as having a "bad attitude." One instance is when a French reporter was allowed into the camp and ask questions, simply because putting the descendant of two four-star admirals on camera would be high demand international news. The "Bug" and another interrogator, "Zorba" told McCain to say that he was being treated well on camera. He refused and was beaten unmercifully. Here, McCain depicts himself as a hard lining, strong and courageous American soldier committed to standing firm in the face of adversity. It almost seems that this difficult attitude McCain vividly describes has begun to deepen beyond dogged resistance to greater loyalty and even compassion.

[17] Ibid., 200.
[18] Nicknames may be characteristic of incarceration humor.

This story, along with the story about refusing to be sent home early most certainly were put into this book to make McCain look like he was a perfect soldier, committed to his country. Although, the end of his five years at the prison camp were coming to a close, many attempts to trade his freedom for a price had come up, and McCain had one foot out of the door. Peace between the Vietnamese and America came on 8 January 1973. Hao Lo released many prisoners, including John McCain on 15 March. He describes the experience of being let free as lacking the drama he had expected it to have seeming "somewhat anticlimactic."[19]

Toward the end of the book, McCain seems to slip seemingly into a form of nonchalant egotism, describing the POW experience as ". . . a formative experience . . . that changed him in significant ways for the better."[20] On the other hand McCain states, ". . . but I knew that life promised other adventures and, impatient by nature, I hurried toward them."[21] The final line of the book also states, "I held on to the memory, left the bad behind, and moved on."[22]

Conclusion

The overall objective John McCain seems to be presenting here is how he grew out of a lifestyle of resistance and a consistent "bad attitude" to being a morally upright and courageous soldier. McCain begins by describing in much detail what a good officer is, by describing what he felt were perfect examples; his father and grandfather. From there he attempts to correlate the two with himself by including many examples of what a good solider would do under the pressure of torture, food and sleep deprivation, etc. By tailoring his story and leaving the reader much to be imagined about the actual POW experience, John McCain was able to make himself out to be the epitome of a solider and officer, falling right in line, and filling the shoes of many generations past.

---

[19] McCain, 343.
[20] Ibid., 347.
[21] Ibid., 347.
[22] Ibid., 349.

Books Cited

Allen, Ethan. *Narrative of Colonel Allen's Captivity* . . . . Philadelphia: Robert Bell, 1779.
Allen, Ethan. *The Narrative of Colonel Ethan Allen*. New York: Corinth Books, Inc., 1961.
Alter, Robert. *The Art of Biblical Narrative*. New York: Basic Books, Inc., Publishers, 1981.
American National Biography. Eds. John A. Garraty and Mark C. Carnes, 24 vols. New York: Oxford University Press, 1999.
Arch, Stephen Carl. *After Franklin: The Emergence of Autobiography in Post-Revolutionary America 1780–1830*. Hanover and London: University Press of New England, 2001.
Berry, William A. with James Edwin Alexander. *Prisoner of the Rising Sun*. Norman: University of Oklahoma Press, 1993.
Bjorklund, Diane. *Interpreting the Self: Two Hundred Years of American Autobiography*. Chicago: University of Chicago Press, 1998.
Boyd, Bell. *Bell Boyd in Camp and Prison*. Baton Rouge: Louisiana State University Press, 1998.
Clark, Albert P. *33 Months as a POW in Stalag Luft III: A World War II Airman Tells His Story*. Golden, CO.: Fulcrum Publishing, 2003.
Coyle, William. *Ohio Authors and Their Books: Biographical Data and Selective Bibliographies for Ohio Authors, Native and Resident, 1796–1950*. Cleveland: World Publishing Co, 1962.
Danner, Dorothy Still. *What a Way to Spend a War* . . . . Annapolis: Naval Institute Press, 1995. The paper cites this edition.
Danner, Dorothy Still. *What a Way to Spend a War* . . . . Thorndike, MA: G. K. Hall & Co., 1997. The Introduction cites this edition.
Dean, William F. *General Dean's Story as told as to William L. Worden* . . . . New York: The Viking Press, 1954.
Denton, Jeremiah A. Jr. with Ed Brandt. *When Hell Was in Session*. New York: Reader's Digest Press, 1976.
Ditsky, John. "The Yankee Insolence of Ethan Allen." *Canadian Review of American Studies* 1, no.1. (1970): 32–38.
Doyle, Robert C. *Voices from Captivity: Interpreting the American POW Narrative*. Lawrence: University of Kansas Press, 1994.
Fabian, Ann. *The Unvarnished Truth: Personal Narratives in Nineteenth-Century America*. Berkeley: University of California Press, 2000.
Gue, Benjamin F. *History of Iowa* IV (1903) http://iagenweb.org/civilwar/biographies/biographies.html.
Hall, James Norman. *Flying with Chaucer*. Boston: Houghton Mifflin, 1930.
Hall, James Norman. *My Island Home*. Boston: Little Brown & Company, 1952.
Hobson, Richmond P. "The Sinking of the 'Merrimac.'" *The Century Magazine* 57 (February 1899).
Hobson, Richmond P. *The Sinking of the "Merrimac,"* with an Introduction and Notes by Richard W. Turk. Annapolis: Naval Institute Press, 1987.
Hyde, Solon. *A Captive of War* . . . . New York: McClure, Phillips & Co., 1900.

Books Cited

Hynes, Samuel. *The Soldiers' Tale: Bearing Witness to Modern War.* New York: Penguin Books, 1998.

King, John H. *Three Hundred Days in a Yankee Prison* . . . . Atlanta: Jas P. Davis, 1904. http://catalog.loc.gov/cgibin/Pwebrecon.cgi?Search%5FArg=king%2C%20john%20h&Search%5FCode=NAME%5F&CNT=25&PID=17177&BROWSE=4&HC=1&SID=1

Lejeune, Philippe. "The Autobiographical Pact," in *On Autobiography,* ed. John Paul Eakin, trans. Katherine Leary. Minneapolis: University of Minnesota Press, 1989.

McCain, John with Mark Salter. *Faith of My Fathers.* New York: Random House, 1999.

McCain, John with Mark Salter. *Worth The Fighting For: A Memoir.* New York: Random House, 2002.

The Oxford Dictionary of the Christian Church. Eds. F. L. Cross and E. A. Livingstone, 3rd ed. Oxford: Oxford University Press, 1997.

Ranke, Leopold von. "Preface:" *Histories of the Latin and Germanic Peoples from 1494–1514,* trans. Fritz Stern, in *The Varieties of History from Voltaire to the Present,* ed. Fritz Stern. New York: Vintage Books, 1973.

[Scott, John H.] *Encarnacion Prisoners* . . . . Louisville: Prentice and Weissinger, 1848.

Shephard, Ben. *A War of Nerves: Soldiers and Psychiatrists in the Twentieth Century.* Cambridge: Harvard University Press, 2001.

Sigaud, Louis A. *Belle Boyd Confederate Spy.* Richmond: Dietz Press, 1944.

Smith, Sidonie and Julia Watson. *Reading Autobiography: A Guide for Interpreting Life Narratives.* Minneapolis: University of Minnesota Press, 2001.

Stearns, Amos E. *Narrative of Amos E. Stearns* . . . . Worcester: Franklin P. Rice, Publisher, 1887.

Stearns, Amos E. *The Civil War Diary of Amos E. Stearns, a Prisoner at Andersonville.* Ed. Leon Basile. East Brunswick, NJ: Associated University Presses, 1981.

Sturr, Robert Doddridge, "Soldiers' Stories of the American Revolution: Autobiographies, Politics, and the Patriotic Ideal, 1775–1830" Ph.D. Dissertation, University of Southern California, 1998.

Story of Company A, Twenty-Fifth Regiment, Massachusetts Volunteers. Comp. Samuel Putnam. Worcester, Mass: Putnam, Davis and Co., 1886.

Vernon, Alex. "No Genre's Land: The Problem of Genre in War Memoirs and Military Autobiography" in *Arms and the Self: War, the Military, and Autobiographical Writing,* ed. Alex Vernon. Kent, OH: Kent State University Press, 2005.

Webster, Charles Clarence. *Sir Brook Watson friend of the Loyalists, first agent of New Brunswick in London.* Sackville: New Brunswick, Mount Allison University, 1924.

Williams, Daniel E. "Zealous in the Cause of Liberty: Self-Creation and Redemption in the Narrative of Ethan Allen." *Studies in 18th Century Culture,* 19 (1990): 325–47.

Wyeth, Dr. John A. "Cold Cheer at Camp Morton." *The Century Magazine* (April 1891).

Selected Sources Consulted

America History and Life, ABC Clio

Atlanta Journal Constitution archives online, ProQuest

Documenting the American South, University of North Carolina

Early American Newspapers, Series I, 1690–1876, Newsbank/Readex

Google

Hall, James Norman Museum. http://www.jamesnormanhallhome.pf/indexen.html

Historical New York Times, ProQuest

LexusNexus, Legal Research

Making of America

MLA International Bibliography, First Search

Oral Histories—U.S. Navy Nurse Prisoner of War in the Philippines, 1942–1945. http://www.history.navy.mil/faqs/faq87-3f.htm

Wikipedia